CHANDLER PARK DRIVE

A novel

By MICHAEL C. LEE

CHANDLER PARK DRIVE

This book is a work of fiction. References to real people, organizations, establishments, events, or venues are intended only to provide a sense of authenticity, and are used fictitiously. All other characters, names, dialogue and incidents, are drawn from the author's imagination. Any resemblance to actual events, locales, or persons, living or dead, is purely coincidental.

CHANDLER PARK DRIVE Copyright © 2005 by Michael C. Lee. All rights reserved. Printed in the United States of America. No part of this book may be used or reproduced in any manner whatsoever without written permission except in the case of brief quotations used in critical articles and reviews. For more information address publisher, Michael C. Lee, P.O. Box 241605, Detroit, MI 48224, or www.mikeleebooks.com

SECOND EDITION

Library of Congress Control Number: 2005901593

ISBN   0-9766830-0-8 (paperback)

MICHAEL LEE

*This book is dedicated to the memories of all the Detroit Police Officers
who have made the ultimate sacrifice in the line of duty*

CHANDLER PARK DRIVE

ACKNOWLEDGEMENTS

I would first like to give praise to God for bestowing me with a gift that I can share with the rest of the world. To my parents, James and Verdell Lee: thank you for always believing and trusting in me. I'll never be able to repay you for all of the sacrifices that you made for us (but I'll keep trying). To my siblings, Mark, Terri, Cliff, Lisa, Michelle, and Barbara (R.I.P.): you know that I love you all (and your kids). To my wife, Erika, thank you for your love and support, and most of all, for giving birth to the greatest inspiration in my life, Micah Michelle Lee.

To all of my friends, co-workers and relatives who have been sources of strength in my life: thank you. A very special thanks to the following persons: Gang Squad (4 Life), Robert Moore, Eugene Sewell, Marcus Haskin (you knew 'it had to happen'), Deneal Mitchell, Bertram Marks (my agent), the First Place Lounge crew, The Inspiration Book Club, Detroit, MI, Elmore Leonard (I took your advice), Gary Hardwick (I took your advice, too), Elizabeth Atkins (you're da greatest), Kimberly Craig (a very special "nooz" girl), Kathy King, Richard "Cadillac" Shelby, and Virgil Washington (you ain't know it was gon' be like this, did ya?), and finally, to all of Detroit's Finest: Be safe, Be professional, and most importantly, just "Be".

MICHAEL LEE

ONE

DENARD HAD DONE THIS 85 or 90 times before. The boss had gave him the loot at the office. The briefing was held at the station and, as usual, Jason was given the assignment of driving him up. However, for some strange reason, this particular deal seemed like anything but routine. Perhaps this eerie feeling was attributable to the lateness of the hour, and the accompanying darkness. Or maybe it was the unseasonably frigid 40° weather. One factor dwarfed all of the others, though. No one from the division had ever gotten a buy out of this place. That mere fact, alone, made the operation an ill-prepared one. In any event, Denard had accepted the task and it was time to get busy.

"You guys have got a green light," exclaimed the sergeant's voice over the hand-held police radio.

Jason quickly picked up the radio and responded, "Okay. Give us a couple of minutes."

CHANDLER PARK DRIVE

Jason, who was driving the older model Buick sedan, turned to his lone passenger, Denard, and stated, "Be careful, dog."

"Ain't no question," Denard, abruptly, replied.

Jason cautioned him, not out of a sense of obligation or because he lacked confidence in Denard's capabilities, but simply because he was genuinely concerned about his partner's well being. Hell, he liked the guy. The two have been partners for two years.

Jason knew, only too well, how dangerous undercover buys were for he had made just as many as Denard. He often reflected on an incident that had occurred two and a half years earlier when another officer and close friend of his had been killed making a buy. The officer opted to make the half-kilo of cocaine buy without a partner present. During the ensuing melee, Jason listened helplessly over the radio while his friend was being fatally shot by the dope man. It was a classic rip-off case. Once the dope man realized the money was present, he shot the officer in the head, took the money, and tried to make good his escape. The other officers on the scene killed the dope man during the hysteria, but that served as little consolation. Jason never wanted to relive that horrid night again.

Jason and Denard finally arrived at the target street. It seemed the closer they got to the street, the more nervous Denard became. No matter how many times Denard had done this, he was jittery each time. For him, the anticipation manifested itself in a most profound way. He'd develop a pain in his stomach similar to that associated with diarrhea. They turned onto the street.

"Damn, man. Ain't *this* a bitch," proclaimed Denard. "As if it ain't dark enough out here, the fuckin' street lights are out."

Almost immediately, they were at the target house, a white frame, run-down, 2-story structure between two vacant lots in a really seedy part of southwest Detroit, off Michigan Avenue. Without warning, Denard exited the vehicle and Jason began the play-by-play on the radio.

"Friday to Slickster. The UC is out of the car and approaching the target location," Jason informed.

"10-4," a voice replied.

"The UC is in front of the target location. He's having a conversation with a black male. I'll let you know if anything changes," Jason said.

"10-4," the voice again replied.

In the meantime, Denard (or Daddy-O, as he was code named by his peers) is deep into his character. As Daddy-O approached the location, a slender black guy wearing a blue Used Jean hook-up with red and white Nikes, and a chubby Mexican kid wearing a red bandana, sweatshirt, saggy black denims and work boots. Both, who looked to be in their late teens, stepped from the front porch, meeting him in the front yard.

"What you need?" the fat boy asked.

This is where the drama started. Denard knew that it was all ad-lib from this point on. Since there was

CHANDLER PARK DRIVE

no existing intelligence on this place, he quickly improvised.

"Let me get two," he replied.

"Two what?" demanded the fat boy, who couldn't have been more than 16 years old.

"Two dimes," Denard replied, without hesitation.

"I got this, dog," remarked the taller, slim boy to the fat boy. He couldn't have been more than 18 years old himself.

Denard promptly focused his attention on the tall boy. As soon as Denard looked the young man over, he realized that the youth was holding a large frame blue steel revolver in his right hand. Obviously, the boy had been holding the gun all along because now he was placing it in his waistband. A brief moment of fear was now in remission once the boy had put the gun away.

The tall, slim fellow removed a clear plastic sandwich bag from his pants pocket. The bag was so full of crack that Denard salivated at the prospect of confiscating it. The boy reached in the bag and retrieved four packs of crack.

"We ain't got no dimes, today. But I can give your four nice nicks for a twinky," he said.

Daddy-O exchanged the twenty-dollar bill for the goods and thought to himself, *gotcha*.

"Alright, I'll holler at you later," Denard exclaimed as he returned to his car.

"I have the UC back with me," Jason stated into the radio.

Denard entered the car, grabbed the radio and reported.

"Daddy-O to Slickster. The deal is down."

"Okay," Slickster replied. "Give us a description."

"The player is a black male, 6'1", slim build, 18 years old, dark complexion, wearing a blue Used hookup," Denard responded. "He's on full. Crack. Be careful. He's armed with a blue steel revolver."

"Got it," the sergeant then responded. "We're rollin' in right now. Try to keep an eye on him if you can."

Jason and Denard both knew that keeping this guy under surveillance was going to be almost impossible without blowing their cover or spooking the seller. Because of the location of the house, Jason knew that there was only one place for the seller to run when the arrest team arrived. Therefore, he parked the next street over, directly behind the target house.

A minute of waiting hadn't gone by when Jason and Denard suddenly heard a bunch of garbled phrases being shouted over the radio. Their adrenaline was flowing because these familiar sounds were indicative of a foot chase. Seconds later, the tall slim seller ran from between the houses, as anticipated. Denard had a strong urge to jump out and catch the guy himself, fearing that all of his hard and dangerous work would be in vain if the guy escaped. However, he maintained his position, and the seller doubled back and found himself captive in the arresting grasps of Pounder, a 5'10", 185 lb. cop who has the speed of Barry Sanders and the hands of Jerry Rice. Pounder was a former Cass Tech

CHANDLER PARK DRIVE

High football standout, and seldom did he allow a fleeing felon to escape in a foot pursuit.

Pounder forced the guy to the ground at gunpoint, handcuffed him and patted him down.

"Heeeyyyy... what you got here, baby boy?" Pounder asked, as he snatched the .38 caliber blue steel revolver from the boy's waistband. "You plan on killing somebody?"

"Naw, man! I ain't did nothin'!" the youth, angrily, responded. He was breathing heavily.

"Get up," Pounder ordered.

Pounder then searched the boy and took a clear plastic sandwich bag from his pants pocket. The bag contained enough crack cocaine to have kept the young man busy until the wee hours of the morning. As the bag was removed from the boy's pocket, a look of hopelessness and despair came over his face.

Pounder escorted the young man and his wares to the raid van parked at the target location. Pounder began to collect preliminary information from the boy in the van while the remainder of the team dealt with the fat Mexican and the crackheads inside of the house.

"Daddy-O, we got your man," Pounder transmitted over the radio.

Denard breathed a sigh of relief. "Did you find the dope and the gun?" he asked.

"That's a big 10-4," Pounder replied, with the zeal of a hunter who'd captured prize game.

Jason then held out his hand to Denard, looking for some "dap." Denard, gladly, obliged, slapping Jason's hand with his own.

MICHAEL LEE

"We'll meet you at the station," Denard said into the radio as they departed from the scene.

CHANDLER PARK DRIVE

TWO

4th **PRECINCT STATION. THIS WAS THE** oldest of Detroit's 13 precinct edifices. Cracked, peeling paint decorated the walls. The outmoded floor tile no longer had recognizable color to it. Most of the offices and rooms were dimly lit by a single 150-watt light bulb. Thought by most of the members of the department to be the retirement station for the complacent and highly stressed, even the personnel projected the image of antiquity.

The precinct commander assigned a small, quaint office to Denard and his crew after the detectives complained about the narcotic officers' misuse of equipment in the Investigative Operations Unit. Members of the Narcotics Division had become accustomed to this type of treatment citywide. One of the reasons was that precinct detectives were usually up in age and, consequently, the most territorial people in the world. The other reason was that most precinct detectives, and some patrol officers, were simply green with envy for narcotic officers. It's common knowledge that police officers, in general, are arrogant sons of bitches, but the narcotic officers were absolute prima donnas.

"Good deal, Daddy-O," one of the crewmembers shouted as Denard entered the work area.

"Yeah, thanks," he, smugly, replied. "So, what did y'all get from him?"

"He had 197 packs of crack and $245," Pounder responded. "He ain't but 17 years old. Slickster interrogated him, and that motherfucker was singin' like the Temptations."

"Cool," remarked Denard. "I'm gonna take the dope downtown. I'll do my report there. It's too fuckin' cramped in this closet."

"Hold up. I'm going with you," Jason stated.

Although the ride to Base 35, the downtown office, was a short one, it often provided ample opportunity for partners to engage in personal or confidential dialogue. Jason had 12 years on the job, and Denard had nine, but they both began working at the Narcotics Division at the same time. Five years earlier, the U.S. Government declared a war on drugs, and the Detroit Police Department followed suit and beefed up its Narcotics Division. Opportunity's door opened and both Denard and Jason left the less glamorous life of street patrol and joined Narcotics.

For Denard, the move was more like a dream come true. He had grown up on the city's east side in a neighborhood where drugs had destroyed many families. Denard was reared in a household where both

CHANDLER PARK DRIVE

his parents were present. His father worked at General Motors, while his mother stayed at home. Two parent households were very uncommon in his neighborhood. The other kids in the neighborhood often referred him to as "rich" and "uppity". Perhaps, by these kids' standards, they were probably correct.

Denard's mother was a no-nonsense type who wouldn't tolerate any form of delinquency from her five children. Thus, Denard and his siblings managed to excel in their school studies and eluded the lifestyles that so many of their neighborhood friends succumbed to. However, Denard grew bored of school in his first year of college and, consequently, his grades were evident of the fact. His parents threatened to cease any further payment of his college tuition if things continued as they were.

Denard knew that things were not going to change. At the time, he was enjoying a sense of freedom that he'd missed in his adolescence. He was meeting and dating pretty girls, which were his *personal* Kryptonite, as well as partying and having a ball, but he realized that if the party was to continue, he was going to have to establish a means to support himself. After working several odd jobs, he learned from a family friend that the police department was hiring. This prospect was right up his alley. This was an opportunity to do something exciting, become gainfully employed, settle down, and at the same time, be in a position to combat the drug dealers and fiends that have ravaged his parents', once pleasant, neighborhood. Denard never

MICHAEL LEE

dreamed that in only four years he would be that undercover officer that he fantasized about being.

Jason, who was six years older than Denard, joined the police department under a different set of circumstances. He had completed four years of college at Michigan State and received a bachelor's degree in marketing but he couldn't find a good paying job in his field. His motivation to join was out of sheer necessity to survive.

In stark contrast to Denard, Jason was committed to a lifetime of bachelor-hood. At thirty-four years of age, he was often ridiculed by co-workers for still living at home with his mother in her posh westside estate overlooking the 10-South fairway of the Detroit Golf Club. An only child, women had spoiled Jason all of his life, and he would have it no other way. The more the merrier was his motto.

Jason, although experienced, approached police work with a more cavalier attitude than Denard. He never longed for the spotlight, nor did he have a personal stake in the crime-fighting arena. For him, it was just a job. The bonus for him was the relationships that he made with the people that he met on the job.

"Man, fuck this shit!" Denard proclaimed. "I hate making these damned nickel and dime buys. Think about it, Jason. We ain't gettin' nobody but these little knucklehead punks, anyway. You and I both know that the dope game is still gonna flourish whether we lock up

CHANDLER PARK DRIVE

these punks or not. And last, but not least, I'm sick and tired of laying my life on the line buying dope when none of the white boys in the division ain't taking the same risks."

"Well," Jason replied, "I'm in total agreement with you on the first two points you made. However, things are starting to change since Commander Jones took over. Those white boys ain't used to having a brotha in charge of the division, and he ain't buyin' that, 'I can't buy dope' line anymore."

"Yeah, I guess you're right," Denard conceded. "But the brothas are still making 70-75% of the buys."

"That probably won't change. This is a predominantly black city. It's easier for blacks to buy from blacks," Jason reasoned.

They were pulling up to the closed garage door of the secluded downtown warehouse building.

"That's why I hate talking to you," Denard concluded. "You're too damned logical. Get your ass out and open the door if you can remember the code, Einstein."

Jason exited the vehicle and dialed several numbers into the keyless entry system and the door rolled upwards.

Once inside of the office, comrades greeted the two officers, and pleasantries were exchanged. In direct contrast to the station they had just left, the atmosphere was bright and cheerful; almost invigorating. Computer generated sounds, coupled with frequent telephone ringing, provided for the only noises other than human voices.

"Tell you what," started Denard, "If you get the analysis on the dope, I'll start the paperwork, okay?"

"No problem," Jason replied.

Denard hadn't been five minutes into the paperwork when the telephone at his desk rang.

"Narcotics, Officer Blake."

"Yes, may I speak with Sgt. Kennedy please?" the caller requested.

"I'm sorry but he's not in the office. Would you care to leave a message?"

"Yes. Please have him call Agent Clark at the DEA."

"Does he have your telephone number?"

"Yes. Tell him that I can be reached at my office until midnight tonight."

"Okay," Denard replied.

Hmmm, I wonder what the Feds want with Slickster, he thought. Eagerly, he grabbed a radio. "Daddy-O to Slickster."

"You've got the Slickster."

"Yeah, an Agent Clark from the DEA wants you to call him ASAP."

"Okeedokee, will call."

Once Denard had almost completed the paperwork, Jason returned with the analysis results.

"Let me guess. It was dope." Denard exclaimed.

"Yeah, yeah," replied Jason. "Listen, since we're off tomorrow, let's go to the bar tomorrow night," he suggested.

CHANDLER PARK DRIVE

"Okay, I can get with that," remarked Denard, "but I gotta get home to the ol' lady tonight. She wants to watch a movie."

"Damn, motherfucker, you ain't but 28 and y'all already actin' like *old* married people."

"Don't worry about me, mahh-fucka. You just try to *get* yo' self a wife. I know how to *keep* the one I've got."

The duo completed the paperwork and departed as quickly as they had arrived. A typical workday had come to a close.

MICHAEL LEE

THREE

KEVIN CLARK WAS WRAPPING THINGS up at the office located in the Federal Building, downtown Detroit. Kevin was a rare find for the Detroit office of the Drug Enforcement Administration. Although he was college-educated, he wasn't exactly what one would consider polished. He was country. Spoke with the twang, chewed tobacco, fished and hunt for leisure. He married his high school sweetheart. The transition from the ultra-rural setting of Spit Bucket, Mississippi to the big city lifestyle of Detroit was not easy for either of them.

Kevin took the good government job because he vowed long ago that he would provide his family with the life that he didn't have growing up, the son of a Mississippi farmer. Kevin and his wife had two children, and a large suburban house. To stay the course, his less educated wife pitched in by getting a job with a neighborhood employer. She worked at a prosthetics factory. Specifically, the company made prosthetic feet. Kevin thought it was the strangest thing that he'd ever heard of when she made the

CHANDLER PARK DRIVE

announcement, but it grew on him after her first couple of paychecks.

Kevin's boss, Stanley Fordham, had just questioned him about the progress of the eastside Detroit case.

"Well, sir, I just called the Detroit P.D. sergeant that you told me to get in touch with," said Clark.

"What'd he say?" asked Fordham.

"He was still out on the streets." Clark paused to spit some brown liquid into a plastic cup, paper towel on the bottom. "One of his men told me that he would have him get in touch with me."

"Good," replied Fordham. He was frowning at the sight of the disgusting plastic cup. "I met his boss. He's a good guy. He says that Kennedy and his crew ought to work out just fine on this deal. Have you gained *any* more headway into where this guy might be keeping his stash?"

"No, sir. But we're workin' on it."

"Alright."

At approximately 11:30 PM, Denard rounded the circular driveway in front of his ranch style abode. Four years ago, he and his wife, Sheila, made a decision to purchase a home in the quiet eastside neighborhood called East English Village. This area was serene by comparison to most of Detroit's residential districts. The architectural makeup of the neighborhood consisted mostly of colonial style homes, with a few ranches and tudors on every block.

MICHAEL LEE

Adding to the area's beauty were immaculately manicured lawns from corner to corner. Even though the homes were moderately priced and owned by middle classed folks, the neighborhood's luster leads outsiders to believe that the area was more prominent than it is.

Finally, as if sheer aesthetic value and serenity were not enough, this neighborhood boasted ten active block clubs, a private security patrol, and twenty percent of the residents were Detroit's finest, thus making it one of Detroit's safest neighborhoods, as well.

Denard parked his car, a black Honda Accord, at the foot of the driveway, exited and activated the car's alarm system. As a matter of habit, he looked over both shoulders and visually inspected his immediate surroundings. Satisfied that everything was safe; he walked up to his front door.

"Sheila, I'm home," he announced as he entered the front door.

"I'm in the den. Come on back," a delicate female voice responded.

Ritualistically, Denard deposited his briefcase, keys and baseball cap on the dining room table before joining his wife in the den. Denard found her lolling on the den's buttersoft leather sofa being entertained by the movie on the 32" screen before her.

Sheila, 27 years old, was only seven months younger than Denard. She was 5'5" tall and weighed a well-distributed 125 lbs. Her skin was without a blemish and her complexion was the color of peanut butter. Although lovely, her shoulder length, brown hair

CHANDLER PARK DRIVE

only paled in comparison to her big, beautiful hazel eyes.

"Hi, baby," Denard said as he entered the room.

She responded with an adoring smile.

"Hi. I was about to give up on watching a movie with *you* tonight."

"Yeah, I kinda figured that. We worked a lot longer than I anticipated. What's on tonight?"

Sheila got up from the sofa, embraced Denard, and softly kissed him on the lips. "Don't you worry about that," she stated. "The movie doesn't start for another half hour. You just go in there and make use of that bath water I ran for you."

"Thanks, baby. Would you care to, uhh, join me?"

"No. You should have gotten here earlier. I already bathed."

Sheila then strolled down the narrow corridor leading to the front of the house. Denard couldn't help but stare, admiring her every move. She was wearing his favorite nighttime ensemble; a short pink, hooded satin robe with matching slippers. Sheila was naked underneath the robe and the satin had a way of clinging to her moist, warm body, accentuating every little curve. She tied the robe's belt just enough to expose cleavage, while at the same time, further emphasizing her peach-shaped ass. As she veered into the kitchen, Denard shook his head and mumbled, "Mmm, mmm, mmm," in mischievous approval.

MICHAEL LEE

Watching Sheila at that moment prompted Denard's recollection of the day they met. It was April of 1986, and Denard, who was an avid runner at the time, was doing laps at a local health spa where he held a membership. He had just completed his first mile around the indoor track when he noticed Sheila ascending the staircase from the lobby. She was wearing a green two piece spandex outfit.

He remembered thinking to himself, *Oh my God. Look at that ass…oooohhhh, and that flat stomach.*

His regular routine called for four miles, but after seeing her, he had a strong inclination to cut the workout short that day. However, he got a grip on himself and just enjoyed the view.

She began stretching on the floor just off the track, so every time he passed by, he had a front row seat. Unfortunately though, after about ten more laps, she had vanished. Knowing that this was the time of year when everyone was getting in shape for the summer, Denard was confident that he'd see her again.

Again came a lot sooner than Denard had imagined. Upon completion of his workout, he visited the spa's juice bar, and Sheila was already there eating a bran muffin. Denard walked up to the bar, which was no more than four feet away from Sheila, and addressed the bar attendant.

"Hey, how you doin', today?" asked Denard.

"Just fine," responded the attendant. "What will you be having today?"

At that moment, an older gentleman stepped up behind Denard and placed his hand on Denard's

CHANDLER PARK DRIVE

shoulder. He then told the attendant that Denard's order was on the house. Denard turned and discovered that the man was Tony, the spa manager, who was fond of police officers and never missed an opportunity to shower them with gratuities.

"Thanks, Tony. I'm just having a strawberry blend, with an egg."

"Anytime, buddy. Anytime," Tony exclaimed. "How was your workout today?"

"It was a workout."

Tony smiled, pat him on the back, and told him to enjoy the drink.

Realizing that this was the perfect opportunity to meet this beautiful woman, Denard collected his drink, approached her table and asked to join her.

"Sure," she replied. Before he could situate himself in the chair, Sheila said, "Boy, you must be pretty important."

"Why do you say that?"

"Well, I've been coming here for a year, and they've never given me a free drink."

Not yet willing to reveal to her that he was a police officer, Denard explained that he was a friend of the manager, who was generous to a fault.

"My name is Denard. What's yours?" He extended his hand for a handshake. She obliged him and smiled.

"Sheila."

"I've never seen you here before, Sheila."

MICHAEL LEE

"Well, I usually come at night because I work and go to school during the day, but since I'm on vacation from both right now, I figured, 'why not?'"

"You work *and* go to school? You sound like a busy lady."

She paused for a moment and took a bite of her muffin, while he sipped his juice.

"So, tell me, what are you going to school for?"

"I'm studying Computer Science and I'm happy to say that I'll earn my degree in June. I work for a software company now, but once I get my degree, they'll upgrade my salary, so you know I'm looking forward to that."

"Hmmm, I'm impressed," he responded.

"So, what do you do for a living, Mr. Denard?"

"I could tell you, but I'd have to kill you," he, jokingly, responded. Her confused facial expression told him that she didn't think it was funny. "I'm just kidding. I'm a Detroit Police Officer." She perked up.

"Wow! How long have you been a police officer?"

"Three and a half years."

"So, do you drive around in a police car? Aren't you afraid?"

"Well, yes I drive around in a police car, but I would have to say that I'm not afraid. I just try to be careful, because I know how dangerous it is out there."

The barrage of questions that he was now answering was part of the reason that Denard was reluctant to tell her he was a police officer in the first place. Most people either loved the police or hated them. Luckily for Denard, it appeared that Sheila was amongst the group of admirers.

"I could never be a police officer. I would be so scared," she said, while shrugging her shoulders and shaking her head.

"I understand," he replied. "It's not for everybody. Listen. Speaking of police work, I've got to go. I'd love to talk to you again, but I don't want to leave it up to chance, so is it possible that I can call you?"

Sheila smiled. "I'll give you my number but fair exchange is no robbery, Officer Denard."

"Oh, yeah. I can *definitely* do that."

They, both, removed pens from gym bags, wrote down their telephone numbers and exchanged.

"I don't have to worry about a man answering, do I?" he inquired.

"The only man that answers my phone is my father. Occasionally. I'm living with my parents right now."

Denard was pleased that he had the telephone number and could tell that she was, at least, interested in him. But, as fine as Sheila was, Denard never imagined that only 18 months later that she would vow eternal love to him and become his wife. Hell, he couldn't imagine that he would be ready to stop playing the field himself, but six and a half years have gone by since he first laid eyes on her and he still found her irresistibly attractive.

MICHAEL LEE

"Honey, are you hungry?" Sheila yelled from the kitchen.

"No. I already ate."

By now, Denard is naked. He stuck his right hand into the bubbly bath water. It was slightly cooler than he preferred, so he turned the hot water nozzle to full blast and sat on the side of the tub. After a minute or so, he tested the water again. This time, it met his approval. He turned the nozzle to the 'off' position, got into the bathtub and just sat there. Absolute solace. He drifted into a dreamlike state. The mean and evil world from which he'd just departed seemed light years away. The only thing that mattered at this moment was the stimulating caress of the bath's warm wetness.

Suddenly, he was awakened from this state of hypnosis by a constant drip of water from the faucet. Denard leaned forward and turned the nozzle marked 'H' hard to the left, causing the drip to cease.

After finishing the bath, Denard joined his wife in the den. He knew that she was not a night person and he had better take full advantage of this rare opportunity to spend quality time together. Opportunities like this were few and far in between. Sheila worked a regular nine to five as a Computer Systems Analyst. With Denard's ever-changing schedule, they seldom had time to meet each other's needs.

"All right, what's on?" he asked, while seating himself on the end of the sofa near her feet.

Sheila retrieved the remote control from the magazine rack conveniently placed at the other end of the sofa. The room was comfortable and uncluttered

CHANDLER PARK DRIVE

with just four furnishings; the sofa, a chair, an entertainment center, and the magazine rack.

"That was perfect timing," she said as she changed the channel on the television. "The movie's coming on now. It's Body Heat."

"What?" Denard, gleefully, exclaimed, "I didn't know Body Heat was on tonight."

Sheila grinned, for she knew this was one of his favorite movies. The movie started and Denard turned off the overhead light to achieve the full romantic effect. The couple enjoyed watching movies together. Neither liked to talk during movies for fear that they might miss something important.

The movie had been playing for several minutes, and was well into the first of many love scenes. Denard glanced at Sheila's face and, instinctively, began to gently massage her right foot; treatment that she truly delighted in. He kneaded the soles of her feet with his thumbs and softly pressed and pulled at each toe. Without a corn or callus in sight, Sheila had the type of feet that advertisers used to sell shoes.

After massaging one foot for about ten minutes, Denard started on the other one. Not more than five minutes later, another steamy love scene erupted on the 32" screen. Denard could no longer prevent the inevitable.

He felt his penis harden as Sheila manipulated it with her unbridled foot. He was no longer concerned about the love scenes on the television as much as he was about creating his own. Practically hard as times in '29 at this point, Denard decided to do some manipulating of his own. He slowly raised her foot to his mouth and, using his tongue, gently kissed the underside of her big toe. Before long, he was sucking it like a lollipop, and did the same thing to a second toe. The expression on her face said it all. Her eyes were half-closed, but she wore an inviting smile. He knew that she was ready.

"Let's go to the bedroom, baby," Denard suggested as he stopped kissing her feet.

"What's gotten into you tonight?" Sheila asked as she opened her eyes.

He winked his left eye and grinned. Without hesitation, she got up from the sofa and turned the television off with the remote control.

As they entered the dark bedroom, Sheila sauntered over to the king-sized bed and dropped her robe to the floor, exposing her completely nude body. She whirled around and found herself face to face with Denard. Denard, who was only wearing a plush terry cloth robe himself, embraced her and began to passionately kiss her. While they stood bedside kissing, Sheila managed to disrobe him.

A few moments later, Sheila stopped kissing Denard and stepped back far enough to look at his body. Butt naked, he stood, as a bead of sweat scurried down the center of his chest to its final resting-place in his navel. She started to caress his chest and broad shoulders. Playfully, Denard pushed her onto the bed, and laid his 6'0, 190 lb. frame on top of her.

Sheila often called him Dark Gable because of his neat haircut and trimmed moustache. She, especially, liked how well he had managed to keep physically fit over the years. The female gym rats marveled at his upper body muscles, but Sheila delighted in knowing that only she got to see how his ass-muscles seamlessly integrated with his hairy, ripped up, thighs. They put her in the mind of two big, black bodyguards, as they surrounded Mr. Johnson, the family jewels and the twins.

As Denard lay over her, he braced his hands against the bed in a semi-push-up, and began tasting her tongue again. The kisses turned playful. They licked each other's tongues like curious school kids. Sheila began to lick his earlobes; first the left then the right. Confident that he'd had enough of that treatment, she began to gently suck on his neck, but as the minutes progressed, she sucked his neck harder and harder. Denard closed his eyes and moaned in ecstasy. Feeling a need to explore his body further, Sheila placed her hands on his shoulders and pushed, softly.

"I want to be on top," she said.

Denard raised up and rolled over on his back. Sheila straddled him at the waist and gazed into his longing eyes.

She continued the action by kissing his chest. She found the fact that he was bare-chested, mildly appealing. She slid her tongue in a circular motion around each nipple until they were stiff as marbles. At the same time, Denard reached down and grabbed her ass and began to squeeze both cheeks, intently.

At one point, he pulled her body forward by her ass until her breasts were perfectly aligned with his lips.

He then began to passionately suck her nipples. Once they were firm, he commenced to flick his tongue across her nipples and lightly blew on them while they were moist. He could almost feel the goose bumps as they grew on her body. At the same time, he never stopped grasping and clawing her bare ass.

Sheila was totally aroused now. She reached down between their bodies and grabbed his rock hard manhood and eased it inside her.

"Oooohhh…baaaabby…baaby…fuck me! Oooohhh…fuuuck meee," she moaned. Her upper body sprang upward and she tossed her head back, closed her eyes and, frantically, began to grind. Her movements were sporadic and uninhibited; varying from a slow and deliberate grind to a sultry frenzy.

Denard breathed heavily and flexed his abdominal muscles as he thrust his pelvis upward with the type of intensity that would have thrown a lesser woman off the playing field. At other times, he simply lied still while she enjoyed sliding up and down on his pole. Although he enjoyed being on top, Sheila's aggressiveness turned him on more than anything. Unselfishly, he constantly fought off the urge to climax, until he was certain that she had been satisfied.

"Ohhh fuck, baby…here it comes," Sheila screamed.

"Right there, baby…yes, yes, yes," Denard responded.

Seconds later, Sheila reached orgasm. She gasped and clinched Denard's body. Almost

CHANDLER PARK DRIVE

simultaneously, Denard exploded, releasing his juices, as his body jerked.

She smiled, rose up and looked into his eyes. As though giving him the seal of approval, she kissed him in the mouth and stroked her hair, now damp with sweat, from her face.

Side by side, the couple lied together embracing one another for several minutes until Sheila turned over to go to sleep. Denard placed his arm around her and they drifted off together.

MICHAEL LEE

FOUR

THE FOLLOWING MORNING, THE beam of sunlight peaking through the mini-blinds covering the bedroom window awakened Denard. Still hung over from the previous night's intoxicating sex, he reluctantly opened his eyes. The other side of the bed was empty, for Sheila had already left for work. He checked the clock on the nightstand and discovered that it was 10:00 a.m., which was considerably later than he'd been used to sleeping.

Today was different. No court. No work. Just time and opportunity to plan for the evening ahead.

Denard got out of bed and slipped into some cotton boxers and walked into the kitchen. A note was posted on the refrigerator that read as follows:

> *Hi, honey. I won't be coming straight*
> *home from work. I'm going to*
> *the hairdresser. I love you.*
>
> *Sheila*

CHANDLER PARK DRIVE

He smiled, crumbled up the note and tossed it into the wastebasket. He was actually relieved to learn that she was going to the hairdresser. Although Sheila was not the possessive, insecure type, she did prefer him to spend his off days with her rather than the fellas. But, for the most part, she was respectful of the time that he spent with his friends, and rarely complained about it.

Denard opened the refrigerator to determine what he was going to eat for breakfast. He was quite adept in the kitchen and had been designated the head chef in the household. Sheila, like most of the women that he'd previously dated, was average, at best, in the kitchen. He quickly decided on bacon, eggs, and rye toast. He washed, groomed, and prepared the breakfast.

Denard chose to eat breakfast in the den, while watching the Jerry Springer Show. Today's show was the typical one involving a situation whereas a man's wife was sleeping with his father, but only after she found out that her daughter was pregnant by her husband, the daughter's stepfather. Just as Denard had gotten totally disgusted with the circus act on the television, the telephone rang.

"Hello," he answered.

"What's up, homeboy? We still on for tonight?" the caller inquired.

"Hell yeah," Denard replied. "Where you wanna go, brother Jason?"

"I don't know. I was thinking about going over to Joey's. It's pretty live on Thursday nights and, man, it be some honeys up in that motherfucker!"

"Yeah, okay. You made your point. We can do that."

"So, how's the Mrs.? She gonna let you hang out tonight?"

"You obviously don't know me by now. I can handle mine. She's happy as a sissy with a bag of dicks on his way to Jackson to serve life!" They both laughed and Denard continued. "Besides, we got re-acquainted last night."

"Okay, okay, Mr. Mack Daddy. I'll see you tonight."

"Later," replied Denard, and the two hung up.

Denard spent a greater portion of the day lounging around the house watching television and listening to music. In the late afternoon, he took a nap on the den sofa while listening to his favorite Babyface cassette.

CHANDLER PARK DRIVE

FIVE

DENARD WOKE UP AND REALIZED that the day had gotten away from him. It was already eight o'clock, so he began to prepare for the evening's festivities. He thumbed through his cedar closet where Sheila's and his best clothes were kept. He selected a pair of burgundy wool gabardine slacks, and a multi-colored sweater. He opted for his black lizard loafers to compliment the dark tones in the sweater.

Before meeting Sheila, he only owned two suits and one pair of dress shoes. He now owned a dozen suits, and a half dozen pair of stylish dress shoes. As many clothes as he had though, his wardrobe was dwarfed by Sheila's, who necessitated the use of two closets to accommodate her wardrobe.

This was Denard's favorite time of year. Fall. A time when the leaves changed from green to toasty, autumn colors. It was also the time of year that best allowed him to show off his finery. The best thing that he liked about the fall was that his birthday and wedding anniversary fell smack dab in the middle; October 24, which he celebrated less than two weeks earlier.

MICHAEL LEE

Denard finished dressing and set out for the club. He was careful to leave several lights on in the house so that Sheila wouldn't have to walk into complete darkness.

He arrived at the club at nine-thirty, and parked on the street relatively close to the front entrance. The fact that he got such a good parking space indicated to him that the crowd was probably light inside. He entered the club and was met by a very large, muscular guy wearing one of the club's t-shirts. The guy attempted to frisk Denard, but stopped immediately after Denard displayed his badge and police ID card. The bouncer then signaled the person behind him, that Denard was clear to go inside, foregoing the seven dollar admission fee.

Joey's was located on East Jefferson and Van Dyke, just outside of Indian Village, a wealthy Detroit community. The inside of the club was designed in new art deco, with black lacquer high chairs, a sunken dance floor, and black glass and mirror cube-shaped tables. The walls were decorated with black, white and silver wallpaper and black and white, large black framed prints of famous black music entertainers.

The club had a state-of-the-art laser light show with racks and racks of mesmerizing lights. The sound system was rivaled by no other sound system in the city.

Denard made his way over to the bar. The bartender was a portly, 40-ish Italian gentleman.

"What can I get for you sir?" he asked, while placing a plain white napkin on the countertop before Denard.

CHANDLER PARK DRIVE

"Martell, straight, with a Heineken."

The bartender removed a bottle from the top shelf and poured the drink, freehand, into a snifter, and uncapped the beer. Denard preferred bars that still did it that way. A lot of the bars were getting into computerized shots, which made it very difficult and expensive for a brother to get his 'buzz' on.

"Seven dollars," the bartender stated as he placed the drinks atop white napkins in front of Denard. Denard removed a ten dollar bill from his wallet and paid the man. He sat at the bar and sipped the cognac.

Minutes later, he felt a pair of hands on his shoulders. He placed the drink down and turned to see whom they belonged to. Much to his surprise and delight, it was Kathy London, a lawyer who he befriended a few years earlier during a trial in which she was the defense attorney. Kathy and Denard had been intimate with each other on two prior occasions, during a brief romance characterized by lunch dates, movies, late night telephone calls, and sex. Their relationship ended abruptly when Denard met Sheila. He had an uncontrollable penchant for the pretty ladies, but he believed in his heart that Sheila was, definitely, the one. So he, conveniently, made himself scarce to Kathy. By the time she'd gotten back in touch with him, he was en route to the altar. There were no hard feelings. She moved on. Even though, Sheila had never met Kathy, he told her all about her right after the split.

"Kathy! Hi, how are you? I haven't seen you in a long time. What's been up?" he asked as they engaged in a friendly embrace.

MICHAEL LEE

"Oh, you know. The same ol' thing. I've just been working. How about yourself?"

"They've been working me like a Hebrew slave. I've been meaning to call you but every time I think about it something comes up," he confessed.

"Sure. I've just come to the conclusion that you don't care about me anymore. You don't take me to lunch anymore. You don't call," she pouted, while, jokingly, poking her bottom lip out.

"What can I say? You're right. I've been extremely neglectful of our friendship, but I really have been very busy."

"I understand. I'm just kidding, anyway. But we do have to get together soon and do lunch. Ooohh, I'm just hugging on you and stuff. Are you here with your wife?"

"Naw, uhh, I'm supposed to be meeting one of my boys here. You probably know him. Jason Williams. He's a police officer, too."

"No, the name doesn't ring a bell, but I'll probably recognize him if I see him."

She sat alongside him at the bar. Denard had always found Kathy to be a very attractive woman, and tonight was no exception. She was a light-skinned woman with a short coiffure. She was wearing a brown, tight wool dress. Although she was only 5'6" tall, she seemed much taller because of her slim figure and the 3" heels on the pumps she was wearing.

"So, what are you drinking?" Denard inquired.

"White Zinfandel."

"Oh yeah. That is your drink, isn't it?"

CHANDLER PARK DRIVE

Denard waved a twenty-dollar bill at the bartender, who came over as soon as he was finished with another patron.

"Let me get a White Zinfandel and another shot of Martell."

As the bartender poured the drinks, Jason approached from the entrance and Denard waved him over.

"What's up, baby boy?" Jason asked as the two men slapped hands. Denard looked at his watch and noticed that it was ten-thirty.

"You think you could have gotten here a little later?" Denard, sarcastically, inquired.

"I got into a little something," Jason replied, with a smirk.

The bartender returned with the drinks.

"That'll be eight dollars."

"Jason, what you drinkin'?" asked Denard.

"I'll have a Lynchburg Lemonade."

Denard gave the bartender the twenty-dollar bill and instructed him to take out for all three drinks. The bartender returned shortly with the additional drink and the change. Denard left three dollars on the bar for the tip. He then directed his attention to Kathy.

"Kathy, this is Jason. Jason, Kathy."

"Pleased to meet you," they, simultaneously, responded while shaking hands.

"Kathy is a defense attorney...and a damned good one, at that."

"I think I've seen you around the court," Jason said. "But I know I haven't had you on any of my cases because I definitely would have remembered that pretty face."

"Thank you," she replied; blushing.

"So, how long have you been here?" Jason asked Denard.

"Since about nine-thirty. Luckily, I had my friend here to keep me company."

Kathy excused herself from the bar to go to the ladies' room.

"Man, that's a fine motherfucker. Where you been hidin' her?"

"Hiding her? We're just friends," Denard insisted.

"Bullshit, motherfucker! There ain't no way you're gonna tell me that you ain't hittin' that ass!"

"Okay, okay. We *were* kickin' it at one time, but that was a long time ago; before I was married."

"Well I can tell by the way she looks at you that you can hit that whenever you want it."

Denard took a sip of his drink, and wondered what it was that Jason saw in Kathy that would make him say such a thing. Kathy returned to her seat.

"Gentlemen, I'm going to have to leave. I've got a trial starting in the morning."

"Awww, I wish you didn't have to go," Denard lamented, "but I'll walk you to your car. Jason, will you watch my drink?"

"No problem. Nice to meet you Kathy."

She waved good-bye.

Denard waited patiently at the door while Kathy retrieved her coat, a long red, wool one with fur trim, from the coat check. He took this time to look her over real good. He wanted to see if he could detect what Jason saw. Nothing magical happened, though. She was still fine as hell, he thought.

"It's cold out. You don't have to walk me to my car. I'm right near the door."

"I wouldn't have it any other way. I *am* a gentleman, you know."

"So, Officer Blake, when are you gonna come over and prepare one of those gourmet meals that you used to brag about?"

"I promise that I'll be over there before the week is out."

"I've heard that before," she said, while getting into her car, a red Lexus. Denard closed her door, and she rolled the window down. "Here is my number. Call me before you come. I've moved. I'll give you the directions. I hope you don't let me down."

"My word is my rep," he defended.

He smiled, closed her car door, and walked away. *When did she write her number down*, he thought. Better yet, how was he going to get in touch with her if she hadn't given him the number? He shook his head and went back inside. Denard rejoined Jason at the bar.

"Damn, man. I was wondering when you were gonna get back. Two or three cuties walked up and gave me the eye," Jason exclaimed.

"Man, you need to leave all them freaks alone and find somebody you can settle down with."

"You're one to talk. What about that fine motherfucker you just walked out? Nope. We won't even talk about that. You heard what the call Slickster got from the Feds was about, didn't you?"

"No. What's up?"

"Well, they're working somebody and they want our crew to help."

"Whaaat? How do you know?"

"The commander's clerk wired me up. Don't tell nobody 'cause we ain't even supposed to know yet."

"Damn, that's cool! I wonder what they want us to do. Oh, this shit is sweet! All I ever wanted to do is go after the big guys and that's all the Feds do. They don't fuck with the little fish."

At the same time, Denard's pager went off. He looked at the pager, and then he looked at his watch.

"Man, that's Sheila. Let me call her back. I know she just wants me to come home."

"Take your time," replied Jason, "I'll just be checkin' out the scenery."

Denard dialed his home from the pay phone. He covered his open ear with his hand to muffle the loud club sounds in the background.

"Hello," Sheila answered.

"Hey, baby, it's me. You paged me?"

"Yes. When are you coming home? I'm lonely."

"I'll be there shortly, baby."

"Thanks. Bye."

"Bye, bye, babe."

He hung up the phone and re-entered the bar.

"Just like I said. That was Sheila, man. I've gotta be leaving pretty soon."

CHANDLER PARK DRIVE

"Okay, dog." Jason replied. "Just be on time for work tomorrow. I'm making a buy at that apartment building on Dexter. Will you drive me up?"

"Wait a minute," Denard said, with a puzzled look on his face. "Ain't that the same joint that we ran up in about two weeks ago when I made the buy and we locked up that young boy?"

"Exactly. The SOI got another buy out of there today, though. I guess they're back in business," Jason explained.

"Man, these fools just don't get enough, do they?" He finished the last of his cognac and beer. "Well, anyway. I'll drive you up. That goes without saying. What time do we start tomorrow?"

"We're starting at two o'clock 'cause the lieutenant scheduled a meeting between the Feds and our crew at seven. That way, we can have our raid out of the way."

"All right, slice. I'll holler at you tomorrow. I've got court in the morning, so I might be a little late for work."

"Cool. I'll let Slick know," Jason assured.

With that, they parted ways.

Denard arrived home shortly after midnight. The exterior lights were on and Sheila was fast asleep. Denard quietly undressed and got into bed; careful not to wake her up.

At seven o'clock the next morning, the alarm clock sounded off. Sheila sprang up. Denard was comatose. En route to the bathroom, her feet got

44

tangled up in his pants that he dropped on the floor before getting into bed last night. Irritated by his sloppiness, she reached down and snatched them up to move them to the paisley chaise. She grabbed them by the hem, and a wallet and a piece of paper fell to the floor. She put the wallet in the pants and tossed them. She moved from the bedroom to the bathroom, turned on the light and eyed the paper. "Hmm, Kathy." And a telephone number.

Who in the hell is Kathy, she first thought. Then she realized that Kathy could be anybody, in his line of work. This was probably some female snitch or a cop or something. Just in case, she committed the number to memory before putting it back in his pants. Her only thought as she brushed her teeth and washed up was *who in the hell is Kathy.* She wanted to abandon this silly notion that Denard was doing something that he shouldn't, but it was hard.

She knew that, even though Denard was a good man, his father didn't set a good example for him growing up. In the back of her mind, she feared that Denard might take on some of his father's wicked ways. Denard shared horror tales with her about his father's womanizing; cheating on his mother. Sheila couldn't figure out why and how Vency, Denard's mother, had managed to stay married to such a man. Denard believed that his parents were just two people that didn't believe in divorce. On occasion, he even expressed concern that he, too, might pick up some of his father's ways, but vowed to fight off any urge.

CHANDLER PARK DRIVE

Sheila's thoughts had gotten the best of her and time had gotten away. It was eight o'clock. Time to wake Denard for court. Dutifully, she did, never mentioning the telephone number. It was two hours later that Sheila had an, Aha! Moment. While seated at her desk, she remembered that Denard had just broke up with a girl named Kathy London before they met. Could *that* be who's number it is, she wondered. Just to maintain her sanity, she told herself that she would call the number, just to see what happens. No big deal. If a female answers, she'd just feign a wrong number. She just wanted to see what Kathy sounded like. After a few deep breaths, she dialed the number from her desk. It rang three times before the following message played:

Hello. You've reached Kathy London. Leave a message. Have a blessed day.

She slammed the telephone down immediately. Sheila's heart raced at what the female's voice said. The words 'Kathy London' couldn't have hit her any harder, than if they *were* a ton of bricks falling on her. She took a few more deep breaths and tried to think rationally. *There could be thousands of legitimate reasons why they are in touch with each other*, she thought. She also wondered how long they have actually been in touch with each other. Why hadn't Denard mentioned speaking to her recently, if it was innocent? There was no end to the questions, and very few answers. By the end of the day, Sheila had decided what the best course of action was for her. She *had* to give Denard the benefit of the doubt. Nonetheless, she dialed a telephone number that she'd found in a local directory.

"Hello. Dukes," said the person on the other end of the phone.

CHANDLER PARK DRIVE

SIX

AT 1:30 PM, DENARD ARRIVED AT BASE 35 considerably earlier than he had anticipated. The day in court turned out to be a very short one. Apparently, the defendant wasn't too confident in his defense attorney's strategy. Consequently, he opted for the "no show" strategy. This didn't go over well with the judge, though; who assessed a stiff penalty for failing to appear.

When Denard entered the work area, he found that he was the first member of his crew to arrive. As Denard sat at his desk and checked his personal mailbox for court subpoenas and other inter-department mail, his sergeant, Terrence Kennedy, or 'Slickster' as he is called by his co-workers, entered the office.

"What's up, Slickster?"

"Hi. How's it going," Slickster replied.

"Oh, you know. Everythang's chicken but da bone," responded Denard. "Jason told me last night that we're going back over on Dexter."

"That's right. An SOI got a buy out of there last night for us," Slickster explained.

MICHAEL LEE

"Are they selling from the same apartment that they were selling from before?"

"No. They moved to a basement apartment. The description that the SOI gave us of the seller is different from the last time, too, but the SOI is certain that it's the same operation."

One by one, the rest of the crew began to file into the work area. First came Pounder, then Jason. 'Too Sweet' and 'F.A.' were the last to arrive.

Too Sweet, the only non-black on the crew, is a 33-year old Hispanic male with 10 years on the police department. He was code named 'Too Sweet' because of his penchant for the lovely Latino women in southwest Detroit.

The only female on the crew, 'F.A.', quickly fit in after joining the crew a year earlier. She came with the attitude, 'respect me and just treat me as you would treat each other'. The men on the crew immediately took advantage of the invitation and code named her 'F.A.', as a crew joke, but the name has stuck with her every since. In normal police jargon, the letters F.A. mean Felonious Assault. In this case, though, they mean 'fatal attraction'. About a year before she joined the crew, F.A. had been the target of sexual harassment by a high-ranking officer. The harassment carried on off duty, as well as on duty. The matter concluded with the officer retiring from the department.

F.A. knew exactly what the letters stood for, but was not offended by it. Although the incident with the command level officer was widely publicized throughout the department, no one on the crew shared with non-crew members what the F.A. stood for, out of respect for her.

"Daddy-O, what happened in court today?" Too Sweet inquired.

"Man, that fool didn't even show up. He pissed the judge off, too. She gave him a $100,000 cash bond."

Too Sweet just laughed and shook his head.

"Listen up, folks," interrupted Slickster. "Let's brief so that we can get this raid out of the way."

Slickster paused momentarily to peruse a memo on his desk before continuing.

"We are supposed to meet with the DEA today and discuss possibly assisting them in a case that they're currently working on," he said.

"Awww shit," grumbled Pounder. "It's gonna be another clusterfuck if the Feds are involved."

"Well, we'll see exactly what's happening at the meeting tonight," Slickster assured.

"What time is the meeting?" F.A. asked.

"Seven o'clock," responded Slickster. "Now, go ahead with the briefing, Jason."

Jason was holding a large manila envelope in his hands, while seated on top of his desk. A search warrant was nestled underneath the flap of the envelope on the outside. Everyone on the crew had ceased idle conversation. The shuffling of paper had come to an abrupt end, and each crewmember was as attentive to Jason as a media person is at a presidential press conference.

MICHAEL LEE

The briefing was thought, by most narcotics officers, to be the single most important aspect of enforcement activities. Very pertinent information is disseminated in briefings. For instance, descriptions of the drug sellers, and drug houses are given. Strategies are discussed relative to undercover buys from a location. At a briefing, a determination is made as to what direction the raid van will approach from, what door will be breached to enter the house, what hospital will be used in the event a crew member is wounded, and who is responsible for driving a crew member to the hospital.

Officers are strategically assigned to various positions with specific duties, and contingency plans are discussed. Ideally, all relevant data is disseminated at a raid briefing.

"We're going to 12006 Dexter apartment B-4," Jason said. "The building is described as a yellow brick, four story apartment building. It's on the west side of the street between Elmhurst and Boston. Apartment B-4 is in the basement. It should be the last door on the right if we take the front stairwell to the basement."

"Isn't this the same place we hit a couple of weeks ago?" F.A. asked Jason.

"Yep. Same place, but they moved to the basement. If you'll remember, we went to the second floor last time. Yesterday, the SOI got a buy out of this

CHANDLER PARK DRIVE

basement apartment. The seller is supposed to be a black male, about 30-35 years old, light complexion, bald-headed with a goatee. The guy is supposed to be about 5'9", but he's real skinny. They're selling $10 rocks. I'm making the buy and Daddy-O's driving me up. As far as guns and dogs go, the SOI didn't see any, but that doesn't mean that there's none there."

"Jason, do you have to go inside of the apartment to make the buy?" inquired Slickster.

"Yeah, Slick. But the SOI said that ol' boy had the dope in his pants pocket, and he was in and out of there like that," he replied, while snapping his finger. "Anyway, we can approach from the west and go east on Elmhurst to Dexter. When we get to Dexter, we can make a right and we'll be right in front. I assume we're gonna get a patrol crew from the precinct to cover the rear. If so, they can just stop at the alley before Dexter and take the back door. That's about it. Oh yeah, I forgot. The nearest hospital is gonna be Henry Ford. We can take Dexter south to the Boulevard and go east. Slick?"

"Okay. Too Sweet, shotgun," Slickster ordered. "Any grates on the door, Jason?"

"Negative."

"Good. F.A., you bring up the crow bar just in case. Pounder, you'll be on the battering ram. Daddy-O, I want you on the entry team after the buy. If we're fired upon before entering, take cover, and I'll declare a barricaded gunman situation. If the shooting starts after we get inside, then shame on 'em. Remember…don't shoot unless you have a clearly defined target. If one of us is injured, I'll have the precinct crew convey to the hospital. If something should happen to me, Too Sweet will make the call. Any questions?" He paused. "Good. Let's suit up. We'll stage at the 10th Precinct parking lot. That's not too far from the location."

CHANDLER PARK DRIVE

SEVEN

BOTH DADDY-O AND JASON REMOVED duffel bags from beneath their desks. Jason unzipped his bag and took out a dirty Pistons Bad Boys sweatshirt and a pair of outdated Levi jeans. He got dressed in the grungy garb in the men's locker room. He wiped the underside of a piece of carbon paper against his skin to give his face and hands a soiled appearance. He replaced the expensive hiking boots that he was wearing with a crusty pair of high top Puma basketball shoes. He completed the ensemble with a greasy, beige knit skullcap.

"Damn!" shouted Daddy-O to Jason. "You look just like one of them crack heads! Did you get the buy money from Slick yet?" Jason removed a twenty-dollar bill from his pants pocket and handed it to Denard.

"Yeah. Why don't you go and make a copy of it for me."

Denard took the bill and made a copy of the money at the copy machine. This made recovering the money much easier after the raid, not to mention, the photocopies were often used as evidence in court if the money wasn't recovered.

The rest of the crew was now donned in black jumpsuits bearing light reflective patches that read "POLICE" on the sleeves, chest and back. Their matching baseball caps had the word "POLICE" on the front. Each of them was wearing a black leather belt, which supported the various types of guns, from the .357 Magnum that Slickster carried to the 40 caliber Glocks that Pounder and F.A. carried. Too Sweet's Smith and Wesson 9MM was supplemented by the Remington 870 12 Gauge shotgun that he used as the shotgun man for the raids.

The crew loaded the raid van with the requisite equipment and set out for the staging location. Jason and Denard placed their duffel bags in the trunk of the Buick and proceeded to the area to look things over. They engaged in conversation while en route.

"So how long did you stay at the club after I left last night?" inquired Denard.

Grinning, Jason responded, "Aww, man! When you left, I ran into this cutie I met about two weeks ago at the bowling alley. I had talked to her on the phone a couple times, but you know, last night was the first time I'd seen her since then." More eager to share his experience, Jason became wide-eyed as he continued. "Well anyway, she must've been about that way last night 'cause you know, she was with her girlfriend, who was a fine motherfucker herself. I mean this broad had …"

CHANDLER PARK DRIVE

"Man, get back to the story before you get all off on a tangent," Denard interjected.

"Okay, okay. Well, like I said, she was with her girlfriend, but I asked them if they wanted to go to breakfast. She was like, 'yeah' but her girlfriend said she had to get up early in the morning. Her girlfriend was driving so I let ol' girl ride with me. So anyway, we went to breakfast, ate and talked. Somehow, we got on the subject of sex ..."

Again Denard interrupted, "Yeah right. Somehow. I know *exactly* how. 'Excuse me, but would you have sex with me?' is probably how you brought it up."

"Man, let me finish. Okay, when we left, I was gonna crack on her to go to the motel, but man, before I could say anything, ol' girl started polishin' my knob right there in the ride."

"What!?", Denard responded in disbelief.

"Man, that honey was a pro. I had to pull over. I thought she was gonna swallow but she spit the shit out the window." Jason was now giggling like a teen-ager.

Still in disbelief, Denard inquired, "Now you mean to tell me that this chick just started blowin' you right out the clear blue?"

"I swear to God, man," Jason vowed, while raising his right hand.

"Slickster to Daddy-O, Friday, we're in position and you've got a green light," the sergeant's voice proclaimed over the police radio.

Daddy-O grabbed the radio and was careful not to expose it to persons on the street. "Okay. We're about two minutes away," he said. "I'll let you know. Where do you want me to park, dog?"

"Park across the street. That's where most of the buyers that come in cars park. I'm leavin' my heater in the glove compartment."

Jason produced a shiny, silver Walther PPK .380 and put it in the glove box. Rarely, if ever, did undercover officers carry a weapon into a dope house with them. Depending on the house's protocol, any buyer could be frisked for weapons at any time. Although being unarmed in a dope house, where all of the dope dealers are probably armed themselves, is definitely risky, most UC's concurred that trying to explain to a trigger happy dope dealer why a ten dollar crack head was packing was far more daunting a task. This placed the dope dealer in the precarious position to draw one of two plausible conclusions. First, that either this crack head ain't a crack head but the police or second, that the crack head has robbery on his mind. Denard parked across the street from the building in a position that he could clearly see the front door. Jason got out of the car and made his approach. Denard began the radio transmissions.

"Daddy-O to Slickster. The UC is out and approaching the target."

"10-4".

Jason entered the main door.

"The UC is inside," Denard advised. "Put him on the clock."

"Okay. We've got him on the clock," replied Slickster. "He's got four minutes."

CHANDLER PARK DRIVE

EIGHT

AS JASON ENTERED THE BUILDING, he encountered two black males, each about 20 to 25 years old. Nice sized guys. Looked to be former high school b-ballers, he thought. Jason quickly realized that they were the doormen, or look-outs, when one of them whistled as he descended the staircase.

The building was old, dirty and dilapidated. Jason peered down the hallway as he reached the bottom of the stairs. The hall was long, dark and eerie. The trek down this gloomy corridor suddenly became something that Jason did not want to do. However, he mustered up the courage and began his journey. The carpet beneath his feet was completely lifeless and filthy, littered with dust, chewing gum, and cigarette butts. The apartment doors were inconsistent in style and composition. Each step that he took down this drab pathway seemed harder than its predecessor.

Three-fourths of the way to his destination, Jason had a funny feeling inside and decided to abort his mission. He turned around, and in a more rapid pace, proceeded back to the front stairwell. Jason felt relieved about his decision until, suddenly, a young black male leaped from within a room off the hallway, grabbed Jason by the collar with his left hand and jammed the tip of a blue steel revolver into Jason's left temple with his right hand.

Shocked, surprised and unable to react, Jason looked his assailant in the eyes and discovered that it was the same young man that he arrested in the same building less than three weeks earlier. On that occasion, Denard made the undercover buy, but Jason interrogated the thug at the precinct for thirty minutes face to face. The brief, fleeting moment that Jason hoped that the young man would not recognize him was somberly extinguished when the man looked Jason in the eye and said, "What's up now, 5-0?"

Jason had written himself off for dead. Conscious of the time limit that he had, and although it seemed like an eternity, he was certain that only two minutes had lapsed, which would give this hoodlum two whole minutes to murder him and make good his escape. Thoughts of his mother, other loved ones and his short life raced through his mind. The most profound image that he envisioned was his lifeless body laying on the cold, mud stained floor with a bullet in the head. He feared that in the aftermath of his murder that the murderer would escape and justice would never be served. The mere thought of dying a death so void of dignity sickened him. But in one courageous moment, he remembered something an instructor told him in the police academy years ago- FIGHT BACK! YOU'RE NOT DEAD YET!

CHANDLER PARK DRIVE

Realizing that he *was* still alive and *didn't* have anything to lose, Jason quickly grabbed the gunman's hand and snatched it away from his head. He forced the man into the wall behind him. The man now had his back against the wall and struggled violently as Jason, repeatedly, beat the gun hand against the wall until the weapon dislodged, fell to the floor and slid several feet away.

Jason knew it would not be long before the goon summoned the two doormen, so he fled up the front stairwell as soon as he had disarmed the man. As he took the steps, two by two, he could almost feel himself being shot in the back, fearing that he wouldn't escape harm. Half way up the stairs, he heard the guy in the basement yell to the doormen.

"Get that motherfucker!"

Once he was at the top of the stairs, one of the look-outs, a tall stocky guy wearing a three-quarter length down filled jacket, grabbed him by his sweatshirt and slung him to the floor. Jason immediately gathered himself and jumped to his feet. The other doorman, a tall, thin character, peeked outside through the cracked door. As soon as Jason stood up, the tall guy tried to punch him in the face. Jason eluded the punch and hurled his body into the man's, causing all three of them to fall outside of the front door. Jason purposely did this to alert Daddy-O of his distress.

Daddy-O saw what was happening through his side view mirror. He slammed the gearshift in reverse and stomped the accelerator, causing the tires to squeal. The two doormen reacted to the noise by pouncing to their feet and dashing in separate directions. Daddy-O, desperately, swerved the vehicle backwards. Moments earlier, the crew, which was less than three blocks away, had received the standard half-minute time check from Daddy-O, when suddenly they heard him screaming over the radio.

"Move in! Move in! The UC is in trouble!"

Without hesitation, Slickster sped to the target location, as well as every other narcotic raid crew that was monitoring that frequency. Daddy-O got to Jason first and determined that he was okay. He then handed Jason his gun from the car and went after the taller assailant, who ran between the houses on Boston. Daddy-O drove parallel to the man until the perfect moment presented itself and he made a sharp left turn, threw the car in park, jumped out and chased the guy about twenty-five yards before tackling him.

Instinctively, Daddy-O slugged the guy several times in the gut to take the fight out of him. After the goon appeared beaten, Daddy-O removed a pair of handcuffs from hanging on his belt and tightly clamped them on the man's wrists. He then made the man lay face down on the ground until assistance arrived.

Meanwhile, Jason was now in the company of his cohorts. Jason had briefly apprised them of the situation and was visibly shaken. Even though apprehending the gunman was important to Slickster, his first order of business was to account for all of the crew members. He grabbed the radio from his belt.

"Slickster to Daddy-O. What's your location?"

CHANDLER PARK DRIVE

Out of breath and panting, Daddy-O replied, "I'm three streets north of Boston, west of Dexter. Be advised, I've got one in custody," he stated, after pausing to catch his breath.

A small crowd began to gather near Daddy-O when the raid van and a marked scout car with uniformed patrol officers arrived. The patrol officers placed the man in the backseat of their car as Jason hastened towards the man. Jason collared the man and shouted furiously.

"What!? You wanna fuck with the police!? Huh!?," he demanded as he clinched the man's collar even tighter.

F.A., who has had the task of calming her male counterparts, grabbed Jason by the arm and assured him that harming the man wasn't worth the certain ramifications. Within a few minutes, two other raid crews had responded to the scene, as well as the lieutenant, who was brought up to speed by Slickster and Jason.

"Is everyone on your crew okay?" inquired the lieutenant.

"Yes sir," replied Slickster. "Nobody's injured or anything, but Friday's a little shaken up. A guy pulled a gun on him inside the building and he had to fight a couple of other guys to get out."

"Yeah," Jason interrupted. "The guy who pulled the gun on me is this joker we locked up a few weeks ago."

"So, do you think he recognized you?" asked the lieutenant.

"Hell yeah! He said it. He called me 5-0."

"Well, the important thing is that you're alright," said the lieutenant. "Slickster, have we located the guy with the gun yet?"

"No sir. As a matter of fact, we're about to search the whole apartment building to see if he's inside."

"Hold on," cautioned the lieutenant. "Have you executed your search warrant yet?"

"No sir."

"Okay. I want you to do that before you do anything else. In all probability, nobody's gonna be in that apartment now, but it's worth a try. How many crews do you think you'll need?"

"One other crew should suffice," replied Slickster.

The lieutenant instructed one of the other sergeants to assist Slickster and his crew with the search of the building. Slickster ordered Jason to go to the precinct and prepare his report. Slickster knew that Jason was in no condition, emotionally, to see his assailant so soon after the attack.

CHANDLER PARK DRIVE

NINE

THE SEARCH OF THE APARTMENT building was slow, but thorough. Slickster stationed an officer at each of the building's three exits to cut off potential escape routes in the event the gunman was still inside. Slickster and his crew first executed the search warrant on apartment B-4 according to plan. Pounder forced the door open with the ram and it flung wide open. The apartment was completely empty, with the exception of a broken oven, a milk crate and a four foot long two-by-four, which was obviously used to secure the door, as evidenced by the steel brackets on the door frame on each side of the door. The search of this apartment was very quick, as there was nothing to find.

Slickster then met with the building manager and obtained keys to all of the unoccupied apartments. The search commenced on the third floor, which was the top, and concluded in the basement. The apartments were small, with no more than five rooms. The occupied apartments were either inhabited by elderly black men, who couldn't afford better housing or younger transients, who were strung out on drugs. The very distinct difference between these two residential types was that, although both groups were poor, the old people were clean and treated their apartments like home.

Despite the fact that all of the officers understood the necessity to intrude on the old peoples' homes, none of them enjoyed it. Each wished they could, as if by magic, rid these seniors of the environmental hazards that come with living amongst drug dealers and users. The older folks in the building were most accommodating to the officers and, freely, admitted the crews into their homes. At times, the officers were given information on other drug activities in the neighborhood. One old man even offered the officers a piece of fried chicken that he'd prepared earlier.

The atmosphere was quite different when the other apartments were visited. Some of the folks would be uncooperative for no apparent reason at all. Inside some of the apartments, the officers discovered small children that hadn't been bathed in days. The mothers of these children were, remarkably, young themselves. Consequently, they lacked the basic parenting skills necessary to properly raise kids.

The appearance of almost all of these apartments was unattractive and, sometimes, repugnant. The officers saw things like chicken bones, stale and molded foods, and other garbage stuff strewn about the apartment floors. Children's bed linen stunk from dried urine, while dirty clothes piled as high as five feet in closets and on bedroom floors. The officers felt deeply

CHANDLER PARK DRIVE

for the children, as they were merely victims of circumstance.

Aside from the filthy and grotesque things that the officers witnessed, they saw illegal items, as well. One man had a crack pipe lying on the dresser in his bedroom, that he'd claimed he'd never seen before. In addition to that, empty crack packaging littered the floors of every other apartment. The officers found a number of notable things and obtained, undoubtedly, valuable information, but failed to locate the one person they sought.

Slickster, his crew, and the other crew all gathered in front of the building after completing the one-hour search of the building. Slickster conversed on a cell phone while the others waited. He concluded his telephone conversation and addressed the crews.

"I just talked to the lieutenant at the base," he said. "We're going to attempt to arrest this guy at his house. He lives at 4758 Rochester. That's about a mile from here. His name is Javontay Sims. You all have a physical on him. We don't know if this is his valid address. This is the address he gave us when we arrested him before. We're going to handle this just the way we did these apartments. We don't have a warrant for his arrest, yet. So, we're not gonna force our way in until we are absolutely certain that he's there. Got it?"

All of the officers nodded in approval.

"Sgt. Lewis," continued Slickster, "I need two of your people to cover the outside rear."

"No problem," Sgt. Lewis replied.

"Daddy-O, I want you to watch the front of the house from the UCV."

"You got it, boss."

Slickster went over the pre-raid formalities and the crews loaded into their respective vehicles and proceeded to their destination.

CHANDLER PARK DRIVE

TEN

WHEN THEY ARRIVED, EVERYONE exited the two vans and two officers ran to the back of the house, while the rest of the officers proceeded to the front door. Slickster knocked on the door and was, momentarily, shocked and amazed when a person that he believed to be the suspect opened the solid wooden door.

"Yeah, what y'all want?" the man asked.

"Javontay Sims?" inquired Slickster.

"Yeah, what?" responded the man.

Slickster had no control over what followed the young man's verbal acknowledgement. Pounder and Too Sweet snatched the screen door open and attempted to handcuff the man, who struggled, violently. The struggle was brief and relenting when Pounder delivered a staggering right cross to the left side of the man's face. He was then handcuffed, easily.

An elderly woman rushed from within the house to the vestibule upon hearing the commotion.

"What's goin' on?" she asked. "What y'all doin' to 'em?" she cried.

At this point, the man was being taken from the house. F.A. approached the woman and tried to put her mind at ease.

"Ma'am, who is this man to you?" asked F.A., while, gently placing her hand on the woman's shoulder.

"He's my grandson."

"Well, he's under arrest for assaulting a police officer with a gun."

Obviously shocked and in a state of disbelief, the woman insisted that her son had been in the house for the last hour. F.A. continued to advise the woman.

"Well, ma'am, this incident took place almost two hours ago."

"How y'all know it was him?" pleaded the woman.

F.A. sensed that the young man has been pulling the wool over his grandmother's eyes.

"Are you aware that your grandson is selling drugs?"

Seemingly stunned, the woman responded, "Oh Lord, no he ain't."

"That's right," answered F.A. "We arrested him three weeks ago for selling drugs. Did he tell you that?"

The woman took a deep breath, shook her head and exhaled.

"Ma'am, we're taking him to the 10th Precinct. He'll have to go to court in the morning. He won't have a bond until he goes to court."

The woman wore a blank face and continued to shake her head.

CHANDLER PARK DRIVE

"Okay," she whispered.

She gave the officers permission to search the house for the gun, but the search turned up nothing. Slickster thanked the assisting crew and instructed his officers to go to the precinct to finish the paperwork. However, upon closer examination of his prisoner, he saw that the man's left eye was now swollen shut. Knowing that the precinct desk supervisor would not accept an injured prisoner, Slickster called for a patrol crew to carry the man to the hospital as a police prisoner.

Jason was reunited with his crew at the precinct. Gleefully, they shared the news of the perpetrator's capture and subsequent flogging. Jason was pleased. Even though these officers didn't characterize *this* particular flogging as revenge for the assault on Jason, vigilante justice was normally commonplace behind the assault on an officer. Everyone was aware of the consequences for such actions, but was prepared to accept them. Even though the possibility of being severely reprimanded for beating a prisoner was ever present, most rationalized that such 'street justice' was essential to the restoration of the respect that the police, so richly, deserved.

After Slickster arrived at the precinct, he shed his raid gear in preparation for the seven o'clock appointment at the Federal Building in downtown Detroit.

"Listen up," exclaimed Slickster. "I wanted the whole crew to be present at this meeting with the DEA, but in light of what happened today, I'm just going to

MICHAEL LEE

take Denard with me. You guys knock out all of the rest of the paperwork and we'll do ours later. Y'all can cut out when you're done. I'll update you on the meeting tomorrow. We'll start at four. Oh, and by the way, I'm really proud of the way y'all handled yourselves today. You did a bang up job. Especially you, Jason."

CHANDLER PARK DRIVE

ELEVEN

THE RIDE DOWNTOWN WAS QUIET and uneventful. They made it to the Federal Building in ten minutes flat and there was ample parking out front. As they climbed the broad staircase, a powerful aura befell Denard. In his mind, the ascension, metaphorically, defined exactly where he was in his career. Suddenly, the apex was a mere stone's throw away. Just beyond the glass doors that they'd entered, were a long row of metal detectors; one of which had the words 'Law Enforcement Officers' displayed above. U.S. Marshals dressed in matching navy blue blazers and gray slacks attended the detectors. As they approached the designated metal detector, one of the marshals addressed them.

"You're both law enforcement officers?" he asked.

"Yes, sir," replied Slickster, as they, both, displayed badges and ID's.

"Great," said the marshal. "I need you to secure your weapons here."

MICHAEL LEE

The marshal pointed to a nearby door, which displayed the words, 'Law Enforcement Officers Only'. Slickster and Denard entered the room and secured their weapons in locked gun boxes. The marshals then directed them to the elevators that would take them to the 12th floor offices of the DEA.

Once they got off the elevator, there was a directory, which indicated that the DEA office, Room 1212, was to the right. Room 1212 was the very last office to the right. It was a small office that simply displayed awards, plaques, and memorials. The only person inhabiting the office was the receptionist, a white female, a brunette, in her mid 40's. She greeted them with a smile.

"May I help you gentlemen?"

"Yes. I'm Sgt. Kennedy and this is Officer Blake. We're from the Detroit Police Department and we have a seven o'clock appointment with Special Agent Clark."

"Oh, okay, just one moment."

The woman picked up a telephone and dialed a number. While she conducted her call, Denard and Slickster made small talk with one another, while admiring the many plaques on the wall. Very shortly, the receptionist interrupted them and directed the men to proceed to the opposite end of the hallway, where Special Agent Clark would meet them.

At the opposite end of the hallway was a locked steel door with a doorbell on its frame, and two surveillance cameras mounted overhead on each side. The door opened seconds before they reached it. A

CHANDLER PARK DRIVE

white man in his early 30's wearing heavily starched blue denim jeans and a powder blue oxford shirt was holding the door open, smiling. He was clean-shaven; scholarly.

"Hi. Kevin Clark," said the man, while extending his hand. He had a distinct southern accent and a wad of tobacco under his lower lip. Slickster shook the man's hand first and introduced himself. Denard followed suit. The man led the officers down another long and unassuming hallway.

"You'll have to excuse these inconveniences, but this is a restricted area," Agent Clark explained. "Did the marshals take your guns downstairs?"

"Yes," they both replied, almost in unison.

"Well, if we all agree to work together on this here deal, you guys are gonna be in and outta here a lot, so we'll have to get y'all deputized and get you some ID cards."

Denard smiled, as the proposal was sounding better by the second.

Finally, they had arrived at room 1262 and went inside. There were three other men in the office. The office, itself, bore resemblance to Base 35 in that there were several desks in an open area. That, however, is where the similarity ended. Unlike Base 35, each of the desks had a computer terminal on it. Another distinct difference was that Denard hadn't seen one black face yet. Of the three other men in the office, two were seated at desks, casually dressed. The third man, who was standing, wore a white shirt with French cuffs, round gold and onyx cufflinks, a silk tie, dark gabardine slacks, and perhaps, Johnston and Murphy wingtips. He appeared slightly older than the other men. He was introduced first.

"This is our ASAC, Stanley Fordham," remarked Agent Clark. "Sir, this here is Sgt. Kennedy and officerrr ..."

"Blake," Denard offered, while shaking the ASAC's hand.

"Pleased to meet you, gentlemen," said Fordham. "I'm glad you could come by. Here, let me introduce you to the other guys. This is William Lefkowski. We call him 'Lefty'. This is Dennis Baldwin and his codename is 'Prowler'. Well, I guess we can go into my office and get started. Should we wait for the rest of your crew, serge? Are you expecting more people to show up?"

"Oh, no," Slickster explained. "The rest are tied up on paperwork right now. Some asshole just pulled a gun on one of my guys during a buy."

"On my goodness," said Fordham. "Is the officer all right?"

"Oh, yeah. Too bad I can't say the same thing for the asshole, though."

"Hey, shit happens," responded the ASAC.

Fordham's office was spacious, with a large mahogany desk. The walls were meticulously decorated with various plaques, photographs, awards and certificates. The most prominent one was his certificate of promotion to Assistant Special Agent in Charge. He offered Slickster and Daddy-O a seat on a burgundy, riveted, leather sofa. He quickly excused himself to his

CHANDLER PARK DRIVE

office door, opened it and summoned Agent Clark to the meeting. The director began briefing the guests.

"This is the deal. Clark has a CI who has informed him that this guy on the east side is dealing a lot of heroin over on the lower east side. The only name that the CI could give us for the guy was 'Stone'. Does that ring a bell to either of you?"

With befuddled facial expressions, both Denard and Slickster shook their heads and shrugged their shoulders. However, Denard did interject with a question.

"Excuse me, Mr. Fordham ..." began Denard.

"Please. Call me Stan."

"Okay, sir. I was just wondering what a 'CI' was?"

"Oh, I'm sorry. That's a 'confidential informant'. I think your department calls them SOI's, right? For 'source of information'?"

"I thought that's what it meant. I just wanted to make sure."

"No problem," stated Fordham. "Stop me if I tend to get ahead of you guys, 'cause I do have a tendency to rattle on at times. Well anyway, the CI says that the heroin is labeled, 'flava', and I'll spell it- f-l-a-v-a of 'duh', d-a, month, and Stone is selling it out of a dozen houses on the east side. What else can you tell us, Clark?"

"Only that, uhh, each one of these spots is s'posed to be doin' at least $2,500 a day at $15 a pack. The CI claims to be an associate of Stone's, and says that he can make an introduction to him. Maybe then we can get a few buys into him and possibly find out where his stash is. The CI thanks that this guy is sittin' on the mother lode"

"Well, how do we figure into all of this? " inquired Slickster.

"Three ways," answered Fordham. "First of all, we've done a week's worth of surveillance on Stone's main spot, an apartment building on Lakewood. If we ever decide to take that joint down, we're going to need a lot of manpower, 'cause they're running a tight operation over there; doormen, runners, counter-surveillance people, the whole nine yards. Secondly, according to the CI and our surveillance, they don't do a lot of business with white people, and unfortunately, this particular crew has no blacks. I'm going to need a black UC to get a few hand-to-hand buys into this guy to tighten up our case. I mean, we could try it but if we do and he gets spooked, he's shuttin' down. Finally, if the UC is good, maybe he, or she, whatever the case may be, will be able to find out where his major stash is."

"I can't argue that those aren't all valid points," remarked Slickster, "But why did you pick my crew? We don't have any conspiracy level experience."

"Interesting you should ask," said Fordham. "Your commanding officer recommended you. He said you were one of his better crews. Clark thought that it would be better to use a face that is less likely to have surfaced at this level in another case."

"Well, I guess, my question now then is when do you want to get this started?" asked Slickster.

CHANDLER PARK DRIVE

"As soon as possible. We've been putting this guy on hold until we found a crew we could trust, and like I said, you and your crew come highly recommended by Commander Jones who, incidentally, I have a great deal of respect for."

By now, Denard is chomping at the bit, although his outward appearance suggests that he's cool as the other side of the pillow. Slickster responded to the proposal.

"Well, I've got to present this to the rest of my crew, but right now, I'd have to say yes. Count us in. I can give you a call tomorrow and set things up."

"Great," said Fordham.

All of the men stood and shook hands, jovially, as though an international treaty had just been signed. Agent Clark escorted Denard and Slickster back to the elevator. The men retrieved their weapons from downstairs, and left. In the car, Denard put in his bid for the UC job.

"Look Slick, this shit is right up my alley. I'll *bet* you I can infiltrate these motherfuckers."

"Well, the CI *is* gonna make the introduction, so it should be relatively easy," said Slickster.

"Yeah Slick, but you know that don't mean shit. If them motherfuckers ain't gon' sell to you, they ain't gon' sell to you, I don't care who makes the introduction."

"You're right about that," replied Slickster. "And to be completely honest with you, I don't think you're going to run into a lot of opposition from your partners. I can't see any of them exactly standing in line to do it. Understand that this could be some very dangerous shit. So, as far as I'm concerned, if you want to do it, you've got it but I still want to talk the whole thing over with the crew before anything happens."

Denard and Slickster returned to Base 35. The crew had gone home. Denard and Slickster completed their paperwork and did likewise.

CHANDLER PARK DRIVE

TWELVE

IT WAS SATURDAY, NOVEMBER 7, 1992, three o'clock p.m. A well-rested Daddy-O was the first member of his crew to arrive at Base 35. He could hardly wait to brief the others on the news. Working weekends was a once a month ritual that all crews had to endure. Still, again, even that was better than what precinct life had to offer. In a precinct, an officer with Denard's seniority would be lucky if he got one weekend *off* a month.

The wait for the entire crew to assemble seemed never-ending to Denard. They trickled in, one by one, exchanged pleasantries and kicked back. When Slickster arrived, he made sure that everyone was present before calling the meeting to order. Everyone remained seated at their desks as Slickster addressed them.

"The meeting with the DEA went well yesterday," he said. "It seems that we were selected for various reasons, but mainly because the boss recommended us. The feds have an informant who has turned them on to a guy named Stone on the east side.

He's allegedly selling a lot of heroin. He calls the heroin, '*flava of da month*'", he signified.

"Damn. I didn't think nobody was still usin' hair-ron," exclaimed Jason.

"According to the feds, this guy is making a small fortune off heroin," replied Slickster.

When the war on drugs was declared in 1987, the primary focus was placed on cocaine, and more specifically, crack cocaine. Not only did the law enforcement community key in on crack dealers, but crack became the drug of choice for the fiends, as well. The façade that heroin was no longer in existence was perpetuated by the crack epidemic.

"The DEA says that their informant is close enough to Stone to make an introduction, which is where we come in. They've asked that one of our guys, specifically a black UC, attempt the infiltration. I'm assuming that they must have an all white crew. They claim that their surveillance has produced no evidence that they deal with white folks. Any questions so far?"

"They just want us to make a buy?" asked Jason.

"We didn't go into details how many buys," responded Slickster, "But my experience with the feds tells me that there will probably be several buys made before an arrest."

"I've got two questions," remarked F.A. "Who's gonna be making these buys? And are we still gonna be

CHANDLER PARK DRIVE

responsible for doing our daily raids over here or are we gonna be working out of the feds' building?"

"As far as who will make the buy, there's only one person on the crew that would be considered ineligible, and that's Too Sweet. Whoever wants to do it can, but Daddy-O has already volunteered to do it. Nonetheless, whoever decides to do it, it ain't gon' be no stroll in the park. The feds usually spend, relatively, large sums of money and that makes it a whole new ball game, as compared to those five and ten dollar buys we're used to making. As for your second question, I'll have to check with the commander Monday and see what the game plan is."

"Will we be involved in the arrest when they finally take the guy down?" asked Pounder.

"Absolutely," responded Slickster. "Although we didn't go into great detail about it, I can assure you that we will be involved in, practically, every aspect of the thing if one of our guys is gonna be making undercover buys from these assholes."

Slickster was surprised at how quiet Denard was during the entire meeting. No questions. No comments. Nothing. Just to make sure he was all right, Slickster polled the group a last time before adjourning the meeting.

"Anybody got any more questions? Well, unless you guys are silently objecting to this collaboration, I'm gonna let the DEA know that they can count us in. Let's suit up. Meet me on the corner of Wyoming and Six Mile in the parking lot of Marygrove College. We'll brief on the raid there."

MICHAEL LEE

THIRTEEN

THE CREW, WITH THE EXCEPTION of Slickster, suited up and loaded into the van. Slickster took out an undercover car to do surveillance on the target location. Once inside the van, this group, which was mute moments earlier about the proposition before them, now had a plethora of opinions and questions on the subject.

"So, what's up Daddy-O? You were there. What's up with this shit?" inquired Jason.

"Like Slick said. They want to try to take down this Stone guy," answered Denard.

"Yeah, but why do they need us?" Jason countered.

"Look. I was there. I think they were pretty straightforward about the whole situation. They could've been lyin', but I don't think so. I met their crew. It's all white like he said. Now y'all *know*, can't no white folks spit no real dope game in Detroit."

"So they're gonna use you as their SOI, huh?" questioned F.A.

CHANDLER PARK DRIVE

In response, Denard said, "I don't look at it as a situation that they're *using* me. I just think that a job's gotta be done and somebody's gotta do it."

"Well, you just make sure you be careful, dog," Pounder exclaimed. "I mean, I know that *we've* got your back, but I ain't never trusted them feds."

Those were the last words spoken on the matter while en route to the meet spot. Upon arrival, the crew stood by until Slickster returned from the reconnaissance mission. A uniformed scout car crew from the precinct followed him. He suited up and briefed the crew on his observations.

"Okay, there was one young brother sitting on the porch. He was wearing a red goose down filled jacket. The front door was closed. The back yard is a jungle, so you guys in the scout car are gonna have to get back there quick, but be careful. That's all I've got. Go ahead with your briefing, F.A."

F.A. removed the search warrant from within the large manila envelope. "We're going to 17777 Wisconsin. It's a white frame, two-story, single-family dwelling, located on the east side of the street between Santa Maria and Santa Clara. The seller is described as a black male in his 20's, dark complexion, medium build. He sold the SOI a ten dollar loose rock of crack."

"Do you know if there are any dogs on the premises, F.A.?" Slickster inquired.

"The SOI didn't mention seeing any, sir."

"Okay," said Slickster. "Daddy-O will be the shotgun man. Friday will be on the ram. Too Sweet will bring up the pry bar. F.A., you'll be on prisoner security. Pounder, you back up the shotgun man. The scout car crew will handle outside security. If, while we are making entry, we are fired upon, I'll declare a barricaded gunman situation. If we are fired upon after we're inside, then we'll identify the source of fire and eliminate it. Remember that if you should have to fire your weapon, make sure that you have a clearly defined target and don't touch any of the spent shell casings because we'll have a crime scene at that point. The shotgun man will have first crack at any vicious dogs we encounter. If one of us gets injured, the scout car crew will convey to the nearest hospital, which is Sinai-Grace, straight up Six Mile to Schaefer, Schaefer to Outer Drive. If one of the bad guys is injured, we'll call for EMS. Any questions?" No one said anything. "All right, let's go."

    The crew executed the search warrant without incident. The only person on the premises, a 22-year old black guy, was arrested for possession of 16 rocks of crack. Everyone looked forward to the following Sunday, which had been designated as a 'paper' day. They came in on Sunday, closed a few complaints, updated some files, and went home. The next time they would be together as a group would be Wednesday.

CHANDLER PARK DRIVE

FOURTEEN

DENARD SPENT THAT MONDAY morning running errands and tending to household business. Sheila was at work. It was around midday when he received a voice mail on his pager. He was in line at his neighborhood grocery store. He waited until he got home to check the message.

He arrived home twenty minutes later. He unpacked the groceries and stored them in the refrigerator and cupboards. He suddenly remembered to check his voice mail. His pager only stored messages for an hour, so he dashed to the phone to access the message. He listened attentively, as the familiar female voice recorded this message:

Well, I waited and waited, but no Denny. I guess if I want a gourmet meal, I'll have to cook it myself. Call me if you get a chance. I'll be at home all day.

The voice belonged to Kathy. Her words and tone had a familiar ring to them. He knew exactly what was on her mind. She craved him. She wanted his body. Today. Now. Then came a bout between his ego and his conscience.

He rationalized in his mind that there was nothing wrong with him maintaining a friendship with a woman, despite their past. He tried to convince himself that no matter how attractive Kathy was, he could resist the temptation. After all, he was a married man now. The ability to resist is what separated wild beasts from civilized beings, he thought. Be that, as it may, he returned the call.

The telephone rang three times before she finally answered. "Hello", she said.

"Hi, sweetie. How you doin'? This Denny."

"Whaaaattt. This is a pleasant surprise. I wasn't expecting to hear from *you* so soon."

"Yeah, I'm sorry I didn't come through last week like I said I would, but I'm willing to make it up to you. Today. I've got a few hours on my hands, so I can come through and hook up a gourmet lunch for you. How's that sound?"

"Sounds real good. Do I get to pick the menu?"

"Anything you want," he replied.

"Okay. I already know what I want. I've got everything you need to prepare it here, so you don't have to bring anything. Nope, nope, no. There is something. Would you please pick up a bottle of white zinfandel?"

"Sure, that's no problem," he responded. "But what am I gonna be cookin'?"

CHANDLER PARK DRIVE

"Don't worry," she assured. "It's real simple. I've got some shrimp and an ettoufee mix that I picked up in Louisiana."

"Oh, you want shrimp ettoufee over rice. I can handle that."

"Oh yes," she remarked. "That is so delicious." She gave him the directions to her home.

"Cool. I'll be right over," Denard said as he hung up the phone. He groomed in front of the bedroom mirror and sprayed a liberal amount of Cool Waters cologne on his neck and inner portions of his wrists.

Kathy lived off East Jefferson in The Lofts, which offered a riverfront view. Although the ride from his house to hers wasn't a long one, it was thought-filled. He constantly told himself that no matter how sexy she was; no matter what she did or said, he was going to remain faithful to his wife.

He arrived at the apartment building in no time. He announced himself at the guard shack and was admitted in after a confirmation. Once inside the foyer, an electronic buzzer sounded, allowing him to open the glass security door. He then took the elevator to the sixth floor. Her apartment was 626. She was standing in the hallway when he got off the elevator. She was smiling from ear to ear. She wore very short denim cutoffs, a sweatshirt and sneakers, without socks. A silk headband tamed her, slightly untamed, hair.

"Hi. C'mon in," she beckoned from the threshold of her opened door. He entered the apartment. She closed the door and immediately engaged him in a warm hug. Her radiant smile illuminated the spacious apartment.

As their bodies separated, he looked around and said, "This is really nice."

"Thank you," she responded. "Is that the wine?" She took the brown paper bag clad wine bottle. "Here, let me take your coat. Is it cold outside?"

"Heck yeah. It's about thirty degrees out there."

She shrugged her shoulders, as though shivering. "Ooohh, I'm glad I'm inside today. Well, let me give you a tour of the apartment before I put you to work." With her left hand pocketed in the left rear of her shorts, and her right one extended, fingers spread, she conducted the tour. "This is the living room, of course." It had vaulted ceilings, a portable fireplace, sofa, loveseat, A/V system, and an aquarium.

There was soft music playing from speakers built into the walls of every room. The bedroom was huge. One of its four walls was completely mirrored. The bed was king-sized with pink linen, high posts and a sheer canopy. A large window was treated with wide vertical blinds, which concealed the picturesque view of the Detroit River.

She concluded the tour with the kitchen. "And this is the kitchen," she stated. "I left everything that you need out. I hope you don't mind, but I'm just gonna sit, sip, and watch soaps. Holler if you need me."

Denard marveled at the kitchen décor. From the Corian countertops to the Jenn-Aire oven, this room truly depicted the loft's modernistic design. He didn't hesitate to make himself at home in the kitchen. The food was laying on the counter and the pots and pans hung from a rack overhead. The seasonings, utensils, and other cooking stuff were easy to find. This kitchen was 'user-friendly' personified. He commenced meal preparation.

"Ha, ha, ha, ha, ha," chuckled Kathy, aloud.

"What's so funny?" inquired Denard.

"This guy on the soap. He told his sister that he's against her marrying her fiancé because he feels like *he's* falling in love with her fiancé."

"Damn, that sounds bad as the Jerry Springer show," Denard replied.

They both giggled. Suddenly, the telephone rang. Kathy sprang to her feet and grabbed the cordless phone nearby. She excused herself to the bedroom after a few seconds into her conversation. Denard continued to cook, but after she'd been in the bedroom for a few minutes, he experienced a tinge of jealousy. How stupid, he thought, as he quickly suppressed the feeling and carried on.

Kathy came out of the bedroom and leaned over the counter that separated the kitchen from the living room. "Is it soup yet? It sure smells good."

"Almost," he replied. "It'll be ready in about two minutes. Where are we eating?"

"If you don't mind, I'll set up a couple of trays in the living room. That little dining area of mine just isn't cozy to me. Not to mention, I want to finish watching my soaps."

Without any prompting from Kathy, Denard entered the living room with a prepared plate, a napkin, utensils, and a glass of wine. He placed them on the tray in front of her. By now, she had removed her sneakers and was comfortably sprawled on the sofa.

"Wow! Now that's what I call service," she said. Denard sat at the other end of the sofa and they feasted.

For a moment, the two were silent as they enjoyed their meals. Denard sought her approval. "So, how is everything?"

Taking a second to chew and swallow the food already in her mouth, Kathy giggled and replied, "Oh, baby. I am so sorry. This is delicious. Can't you tell? I haven't come up for air yet. But I didn't expect anything less from you." She took a sip of the wine. "Mmmm, mmm, mmm. What kind of wine is this?" she asked.

"That's B & G Vouvray. Do you like it? They didn't have white zinfandel where I went."

"Yes. I have never tasted a white wine that was as sweet as this."

"I'm glad you like it. I kinda figured you would."

She stared at him; grinning. "You think you know me, don't you?" she asked.

"No," he answered. "I *know* that I know you."

It seemed as though both of them sensed an aura of forbidden romanticism and, almost simultaneously, resumed eating and drinking. Kathy finished first and gathered her plate and glass, and collected Denard's when he finished. She placed the soiled dishes in the dishwasher and returned with two fresh glasses of wine, giving one to Denard.

She stood barefoot and erect in front of him. Her feet were, practically, buried in the thick, plush carpet. She extended her glass outward for a toast.

"To one of the best meals and one of the best men."

Instinctively, Denard raised an eyebrow and smiled. He tapped the rim of his glass against hers. They sipped, and she seated herself next to him on the sofa. She grabbed a nearby remote control.

"Are you watching this?" she inquired.

"Oh, no," he replied.

She turned the television off and played a cut from Fourplay's new CD. "Do you like that?" asked Kathy.

"Yeah, that's cool." He paused. "So, Ms. London, what's been goin' on?"

"You know. Same ol' thing. No, wait. Did I tell you that I was promoted recently?"

"No, to what?"

"The firm that I'm with made me a junior partner."

"Shut up. Sounds like you gon' be rollin' in the dough soon."

"I hope so, 'cause they're working the mess out of me."

Again they sipped the wine. The track on the CD ended. There was a silence before a new rendition of Marvin Gaye's 'After The Dance' began to play. The mood was rapidly approaching the romantic stage.

MICHAEL LEE

Denard realized that the music, the wine, the surroundings and even the food, were a collective aphrodisiac. Suddenly, he was feeling uninhibited and adventurous.

"Let's dance, baby," Denard announced. Without hesitation, Kathy gladly accommodated his request. She wrapped her arms around his shoulders. He caressed her hips and lower back. Kathy closed her eyes and rested her head against his chest and drifted into conscious hypnosis. El DeBarge's crisp and melodic voice was entrancing.

As the music came to an end, they remained embraced. Kathy tilted her head back slightly and gazed into his eyes. Denard leaned forward, and gently kissed her lips. Another ballad began to play and he kissed her a second time, this time using his tongue. She, again, rested her head on his chest and danced.

The song had not yet reached its second verse when, without warning, he heaved her from the floor and cradled her in his arms. He marched her into the bedroom and placed her on the bed. He lied down next to her and they passionately kissed one another. They rolled around on the gigantic bed like puppies.

"Wait a minute," Kathy whispered.

Fearing that she'd lost a bout with *her* conscience, Denard, timidly, asked her what was wrong.

"I've got to go freshen up," she responded.

Having heard this same woman utter those same words on previous occasions, Denard took them as his cue to disrobe. She returned minutes later wearing absolutely nothing. At first, he was stunned until he remembered that he, too, was damned near naked.

"Come here, girl. You look even better than I remember."

Kathy got back in the bed and they resumed foreplay. She had a sweet floral fragrance about her. They French-kissed, while embracing and rolling atop the comforter. She constantly stroked his muscular legs with the soles of her feet. Aggressively, Denard flipped her onto her back. He straddled her at the waist and, wildly, nibbled at her breasts. He slowly moved downward and started licking and kissing her stomach. At times, she giggled and caressed his head.

Finally, he'd found himself at eye level with her hairless crotch. Teasingly, he licked and sucked her inner thighs. Once he felt that he'd stalled enough, he flicked his tongue across the lips of her love box. She moaned and squirmed about in torturous anticipation. Her body writhed from the attention that he paid her clitoris. Looking up, and without stopping, he examined her facial expressions. She buried the heels of her feet into the bed and pushed, as though trying to escape pleasure.

Knowing that he had her where we wanted her, Denard stopped and retrieved that 'just-in-case' condom from his pants pocket. He slid it on and rolled her over again. She got on all fours, spread her legs and lowered her upper torso, offering full exposition to an inviting ass and a soggy cunt. He, gently, guided his diamond-hard shaft inside as her moans grew more intense. With his hands directing her ass movement, he delivered slow and easy strokes before picking up the pace in an alternating fashion. She rose up and thrust her ass backwards, over and over again.

Hissing and panting, she moaned, "Fuck me! Fuck me!"

"Stand up," Denard ordered.

They stood on the bed. With her hands, she braced herself on the wall in front of her, slightly bent. She, eagerly, received him as they fucked even harder now. She finally climaxed. He enjoyed his moment a few minutes later. Afterward, they collapsed on the bed next to each other. The music was still playing as daylight pierced the blinds.

CHANDLER PARK DRIVE

FIFTEEN

DENARD AWOKE AND GLANCED AT his watch. It was 4:30 PM. He had been sleeping for an hour and a half. Kathy was still sleeping. Rather than wake her up, he took a quick shower, wrote her a note and left without a peep.

He was more concerned with racing home to meet his wife. The ride home was agonizing. Perhaps it was his conscience or guilt, but he felt as though a thousand sets of eyes were on him; following him. He beat himself up for what he'd just done. Although he hated the fact that he succumbed to temptation, the sex was so damn good that he couldn't honestly promise himself that it wouldn't happen again.

Upon circling his driveway, he realized that Sheila was already home. Still feeling as though he'd been followed home, he gave himself and his surroundings the once over before going inside the house. He even sniffed his clothes to make sure that no perfume scent lingered in the fabric. Confident that everything was in table order, he went inside.

"Honey, I'm home," he said upon entering.

MICHAEL LEE

"I'm in the kitchen," Sheila responded.

The aroma of garlic, oregano, and other spices greeted him in the foyer as he hung up his coat and tossed his keys and hat. In the kitchen, he found Sheila, donning a white apron, preparing spaghetti.

"Hi, baby," she said, with a gigantic smile on her face. She offered him an embrace, careful not to touch him with her, spice-soiled, hands. He held her and kissed her lips. She got right back to her cooking. "I got home and you weren't here, so I decided to surprise you with a nice hot meal. Where were you? Did you have some errands to run? I see you did some grocery shopping."

Denard was, actually, glad that Sheila was so talkative today. On his way home, he hadn't even given any thought to an alibi but, unwittingly, she had just provided him with one.

"Yeah, yeah, I had a few errands to run, you know, pay some bills and stuff," he responded, trying not to sound nervous.

"I figured as much," she added. "Now, you go watch TV or something. I don't want you watching me cook. You know that makes me nervous."

"Okay," he said.

He couldn't believe how easy that was. He was *certain* that the guilt would be written all over his face but it, obviously, wasn't. She bought it. Every morsel. He was out of the woods, he thought. At least for now. At the same time, he couldn't help feeling like the world's biggest heel. With a lovely wife who trusted

CHANDLER PARK DRIVE

him so much that she wasn't remotely suspect of his unfaithfulness, how could he, he thought.

He really felt bad knowing that he'd just cooked this 'other woman' a fabulous meal while his wife was at home doing the same deed for him. He had turned the television on in the den, but he wasn't really watching it. Thoughts of his wife and the 'other woman' consumed his mind, until he, finally, grabbed hold of himself and focused on TV.

About a half an hour later, Sheila came into the den and announced that dinner was being served in the dining room. He washed his hands and joined her there. His plate had already been prepared for him.

"I hope you like it," she said.

"I'm sure I will," he remarked. "What did you do with my hat and keys?"

"Your hat is in the closet and I put your keys on the nightstand in the bedroom. I really wish that you would stop putting all of your stuff on the dining room table. You know how that bothers me."

In a patronizing manner, he responded, "Okay, okay." In an effort to change the subject, he asked, "So how was work today?"

"Oh, it was fine," answered Sheila. "My supervisor told me that we were going to upgrade our systems from 486 to 586 starting next week. That should make things a little easier for me. How about you? When do you go back to work?"

"I go back on Wednesday. I don't know if I told you, but we're gonna be working with the DEA on this case and it looks like I'm gonna be the undercover officer on the case. The guy we're gonna be working is supposed to be a major player."

"Well, why do *you* have to be the undercover? Why can't somebody else do it?" Sheila asked.

"Honey, it's not a situation where I *have* to do this. I *volunteered* to do it. I see it as an opportunity."

"I know one thing," she began. "I'll be glad when you stop making these undercover buys. I don't want anything to happen to you."

Before he could say anything, his pager sounded off. He looked at the display. "Dang! Who is this calling me now?" He excused himself from the table and retrieved the message. He tried, desperately, to mask his expressions as he listened to the following:

Hi. It's me. I just called to say that I enjoyed myself and to let you know that everything was scrumptious and delicious. The food wasn't bad either. I know you probably can't call me back right now but call me as soon as you can.
Bye-bye

He, quickly, pushed the button on the phone that would erase the message and returned to the dinner table.

"Who was it?" Sheila asked.

"Oh, it was Jason reminding me of a court case we have tomorrow."

They concluded their meals and watched television. To his relief, Sheila seemed to be sleepy, rather than sexy tonight. After his midday tryst, he

CHANDLER PARK DRIVE

didn't think he could muster up enough energy to go again. They'd only been watching TV for an hour when Sheila had fallen asleep. He woke her and they went to bed together. She fell, fast, asleep. He, on the other hand, couldn't sleep. He thought about earlier, and thought about it, until he, too, dozed off.

SIXTEEN

WEDNESDAY HAD FINALLY ARRIVED. The crew met at their base before going to the Federal Building together. They were all excited. Denard, in particular, was eager to establish himself as a 'world class' UC, while at the same time score a significant victory in the, ever present, war on drugs.

They arrived in two vehicles, which they parked over a half block away, due to restricted parking around the building and parking lots that were on full. They went inside, secured their weapons, and took the elevator to the twelfth floor. The receptionist, who appeared to be expecting them, admitted them entry into the DEA office. The agents that Denard had met earlier were in the office, along with several other people. Agent Kevin Clark greeted them first.

"Hi, uh, Sgt. Kennedy, right?" he asked, while shaking Slickster's hand.

"Right," responded Slickster.

"We thought you guys had changed yer mind," stated Clark. "We were under the impression that you guys were gon' be here at four o'clock."

CHANDLER PARK DRIVE

"No," replied Slickster. "We started at four, but we went to our base first, then we came over here."

As Clark then excused himself, Agent Lefkowski approached the crew and introduced himself to everyone that he hadn't already met. He then introduced them to everyone else in the office. After all of the introductions had been made, they were offered seats at various empty desks. The ASAC came out of his office minutes later. He, too, was introduced to the remainder of the crew.

"Okay, so are we ready to get started?" asked Fordham, who was smiling and clasping his hands together. The crew responded with guarded certainty by shrugging their shoulders and nodding their heads. "Sgt. Kennedy, did we decide who's going to be attempting the buys?" he asked.

"Oh, yes. That's gonna be Officer Blake, uh, Daddy-O."

"Great," said Fordham. "Clark's got his CI here now. If you and Blake would come with me, I'll introduce you to him."

The three left the office and proceeded down the corridor to another room across the hall. This room was where they debriefed CI's. It was small, about ten feet by ten feet, with a window. It was furnished with a plain oak table, four chairs, and a telephone with a cassette tape recorder attached. Clark was already in the room. With him was a frail, light complected black man in his mid-30's. He was wearing a Troop jacket, black Swedish knit pants, and burgundy snake-skinned shoes.

His hair was permed, but in desperate need of a touch-up. His skin was dry and ashy.

Agent Clark had an ink pen in his hand and a legal pad was lying on the table. He appeared to be in the middle of a conversation with the man, as both of them focused on the door when the three men entered.

"Clark, Officer uhh." Fordham paused for a moment and whispered in Denard's ear, asking what his code name was. Denard whispered his response to him. "Uh, Clark, Daddy-O here is going to be the UC on these deals."

"Okay," Clark, nonchalantly, replied. "Well, Daddy-O, this here is Red. He's the CI that's gon' introduce you to Stone."

The CI extended his ashen hand to Daddy-O for a handshake. Reluctantly, he obliged. Without being asked for his opinion, Red offered his personal 'first impression' of Daddy-O, as a UC. His voice growled, as though he had phlegm constantly lodged in his throat.

"Yeah, dat's cool man," he said, nodding in approval. "You scraight, dog. You don't look nuttin' like no cop. I'll bet you be foolin' niggas on da screet all da time."

Denard was actually delighted to get a vote of confidence from the CI, but he didn't let it show on his face. He didn't want the CI to think he was soft. Denard would rather be feared than liked or respected by a snitch. It was a control mechanism. Red did, however, turn him off when he spoke the 'N' word, especially in front of those white folks. That was a big no-no in Denard's book, but he chose not to sweat it.

CHANDLER PARK DRIVE

Sensing that Daddy-O was embarrassed by the CI's endorsement, Agent Clark quickly intervened. "Gee, thanks Red, for yer approval. I'm sure that Daddy-O, here, will rest a lot easier now that he knows you 'prove of em and all. Anyways, we was just about to contact his man by phone. Red, how soon can you make an introduction?"

"I can introduce him today if you want me to."

"Well, I don't know. Are you ready for an introduction today, Daddy-O?" Clark asked.

"I don't know. How's this supposed to go down?"

Clark got up from the table and invited everyone, with the exception of Red, into the hallway.

"I don't like to say too much in front of those snitches, ya know," Clark explained. "I thank that now is a good time to bring the rest of yer crew up to speed." Once inside the original office, Clark conducted his briefing. "Okay, guys ..." He paused, smiling. "And lady, what we'd like to do is get Daddy-O introduced tonight. The CI is pretty confident that he can make the intro tonight. Who knows, we might even be able to buy a sample, too. Anyways, if we do this, Daddy-O's gon' be in the undercover vehicle with the CI. Hopefully, he'll be able to bring a cover officer in the car with him. For this first meeting, I don't recommend gettin' outta the car. What you think, boss?"

"Definitely not," Fordham answered. "I'd like this initial meeting to go down someplace relatively neutral. You know, like a restaurant parking lot. Some place public."

"Alright," continued Clark. "I'll make sure the CI knows how we want to do this." At this point, Clark focused his attention solely on Daddy-O. "Okay, Daddy-O, you thank about who you want for yer cover. We gon' provide you with a listening device for the car. Plus, we gon' have our surveillance plane in the air. We should …" He paused. "Did all of y'all bring cars?"

"We brought two," Slickster replied.

"Good," said Clark. "We got three more, so we can set up in the area just in case things go bad. Daddy-O, I'm gon' give you a beeper and a cell phone. You can give the guy the beeper number if he wants to get in touch with you again. If we call you on that cell phone, that means somethin's wrong, so make sure you keep it on at all times. Uhh, that's all that I can thank of. Did I leave anythang out, boss?" Fordham shook his head, 'no'. "How *you* doin', Daddy-O? You got any questions?" Clark asked.

Questions, Denard thought. He was completely overwhelmed. The whole notion of listening devices, beepers, cell phones, and airplanes, even, left him in a state of awe. He collected his thoughts and responded as intelligently as he could.

"Well, first of all, I want Jason to be my close in cover. Secondly, is it possible that they might detect the listening device?"

"Well no, not really," replied Fordham. "Lefty, go and grab one. They don't look like listening devices," he stated, with quotation fingers. "One looks like an eyeglass case. Another looks like a videotape box, and the last one looks like a radar detector."

CHANDLER PARK DRIVE

Just as he finished the explanation, Lefty returned with all three. Daddy-O and his partners marveled at them.

"What about the beeper number?" inquired Denard. "Is there any way it can be traced back to the DEA?"

"We put the pagers in dummy corporation names, which is exactly what some of the dope boys do," stated Clark.

"Earlier, you said that you'd be in place, just in case things go bad," added Jason. "I have two concerns about that myself. Are you saying that you don't *normally* have crews in place when an agent goes under?"

"No, I'm sorry if that's the way I came off, but we always have sufficient cover or we won't do it," replied Clark.

"The other question is do things often *go* bad for an operation like this?"

Clark was prepared to respond. However, Director Fordham raised a hand and offered a response.

"No. For a small operation of this magnitude, I don't expect any problems. However, it's been my experience, and probably yours too, that whenever you don't expect it, that's when things go bad. So, I just like to prepare for the worst and hope for the best."

Jason seemed satisfied with their responses. The rest of the crew seemed, equally, appeased. Assured that there were no more questions or comments, Clark, Daddy-O, and Slickster left the room.

MICHAEL LEE

SEVENTEEN

"DAMN, I THOUGHT Y'ALL WASN'T gon' never get back," complained Red. "If y'all don't wanna do no bin-ness, I can go on to da crib and hook up wit' dis li'l philly."

"Yeah, Red," replied Clark. "I can see you dressed all up for her and everythang. Look here. I want you to call Stone. Tell him that you want to introduce him to somebody that wants to buy a sample of his product. Tell him he wants a gram. We'd like to do it while it's still *some* daylight, and preferably in a public place. Try to give us at least an hour and a half."

Red took on a more attentive posture as Clark inserted a cassette tape into the recorder. Sensing that Daddy-O might not be completely familiar with the protocol, Clark explained his actions.

"We tape every telephone conversation that we have with a potential target." Red dialed the number after Clark pushed the 'record' button. The room was silent as Red commenced talking.

"Yo. Let me speak to Stone. What's up, nigga? Yeah, this Red. Check dis out. I got dis nigga wanna

CHANDLER PARK DRIVE

holler at ya. He say he wanna taste one of dem gram crackers ... Yeah, I told him dat's how much it was gon' be. Can we hook up wit' you tonight? ... I know what you sayin', but homeboy say if it tastes good, he gon' wanna get a whole pack real soon ... Cool ... Dat ain't no problem, either ... All right, we'll see you then."

   Red hung up the phone and Clark pushed the 'stop' button. He re-winded the tape and played it back:

Unknown: *Hello*
Red: *Yo. Let me speak to Stone. (pause)*
Stone: *Hello*
Red: *What's up, nigga?*
Stone: *Who dis? Red?*
Red: *Yeah, dis Red. Check dis out. I got dis nigga wanna holler at ya. He say he wanna taste one of dem gram crackers.*
Stone: *Tell dat nigga one gram cracker gon' cost him a buck and a half.*
Red: *Yeah, I told him dat's how much it was gon' be. Can we hook up wit you tonight?*
Stone: *Fuck I look like, Dominoes Pizza, motherfucker?*
Red: *I know what you sayin', but homeboy say if it tastes good, he gon' wanna get a whole pack real soon.*
Stone: *Oh, so dis nigga's a baller, huh? Okay, y'all niggas meet me in front of Skateland on Alter Road at eight o'clock.*
Red: *Cool*
Stone: *I'll meet dis nigga, but if he wanna do bin-ness wit me, he gon' have to go through you for now.*
Red: *Dat ain't no problem, either.*

MICHAEL LEE

Stone: *Eight o'clock nigga. Don't be late.*
Red: *All right, we'll see you then.*

"Well, y'all heard 'em. Gram gon' cost you a hun-net fitty dollars," remarked Red.

"What's this Skateland?" asked Clark.

Denard chimed in. "Oh, it's a neighborhood skating rink on the eastside. On Wednesday nights, all of the little sack chasers and dope boys be hangin' out there. They've got a pretty well-lit parking lot out front. It should be alright."

With the exception of Red, everyone left the room and returned to the main office. Clark got everybody's attention in the office and started the briefing.

"Okay, here's the deal. It's five-thirty now. We've got an appointment to meet with the target at eight o'clock. Do we have enough time to get the bird up in the air, boss?" Fordham nodded. "Daddy-O is gonna ride to the target location, which incidentally, is Skateland on Alter Road, over on the eastside. We're gon' do the deal in the parking lot. Jason's gon' be close-in cover for Daddy-O. We're buyin' one gram of heroin for a hundred fifty dollars. We'll have surveillance vehicles positioned to the north, south, east, and west of the target."

Denard was now desperately trying to mask his fear and apprehension with a 'cool' façade, but the nervousness had already transformed into a full blown stomach ache, which he knew would remain with him until the deal was over. He selected the eyeglass case

CHANDLER PARK DRIVE

listening device and they gave him the keys to a brand new burgundy Ford Taurus.

Upon securing the car, he circled the block of the Federal Building and picked up his two passengers, Jason and Red. Jason rode in the back seat, allowing Red to ride in the front. Despite the fact that Daddy-O was equipped to the tee, with an impressive supporting cast, his stomach ache just wouldn't go away.

"You ready, homie?" Jason inquired.

"As ready as I'll ever be."

Stone was at home in his apartment with his common law family; a woman and a child, just as concerned about the rendezvous. Stone had earned a reputation in the hood for being a shrewd and ruthless businessman. Although he had not been formally charged with any murders, most folk in the hood believed he was responsible for, at least, three killings. Stone did nothing to change people's perception of him. It was good for business.

Stone got into the game when he was a teen-ager attending Southeastern High School on the eastside. He sold five and ten-dollar bags of weed to other school kids and some, faculty members. His urban legend was born when he forced an eastside candy store owner to let him sell weed and crack out of the store.

The store, which was on East Six Mile Road, has since gone out of business, due to the owner's untimely death. The building sits vacant today. Some small kids in the neighborhood came into the store one morning and found him shot to death. Believed by the police to be a robbery gone bad, it remains an unsolved homicide. Folks in the hood, though, count the store owner's murder as one of Stone's three. Stone's strong-arm tactics became the trademark that led to his empire today.

His ghetto queen, and baby's mama, Tamika, grew quickly accustomed to the lifestyle of the dope man's woman and baby's mama. She realized and accepted the fact that she was one of many women. She also realized that she had seniority, because she was *still* his only baby's mama. Their 4-year old son, Kenyatta, was none the wiser. Though usually decked out in his baby Jordan sneakers, and Pelle Pelle jacket, his innocence was the only thing that brought true legitimacy to their relationship.

Denard looked at his watch and could not believe that it was 7:05. He drove slowly toward the location and took advantage of the down time to quiz Red.

"So, what is this guy Stone like?" he asked.

"What you mean, 'what he like'?" a confused Red inquired.

"You know. Are these some hardcore, cut-throat motherfuckers or what?"

"Put it dis way," Red began. "I ain't never seent 'em kill nobody, but I don't put killin' past nobody in da game. 'Sides, I think dem niggas work for Stone would kill any nigga he told 'em to."

"What's their setup like over on Lakewood?" asked Daddy-O.

CHANDLER PARK DRIVE

"Aww, man. It's some serious shit over dere, dog. I mean, deez cats is da shit. Man, dey got control over dat whole damn apartment building. Stone always have at least two or three armed niggas up in 'ere. He always packin'. If y'all plannin' on runnin' up in there, ya better come correct. Dem niggas got dat place fortified. Niggas got lookouts e'ry where. Whenever y'all decide to hit it, ya may as well call da motherfuckers and tell 'em ya comin', 'cause dey gon' peep y'all from a mile away, anyway."

As if designed to break Red's ardent stride, the cellular phone rang and Daddy-O answered it.

"Hello."

"Daddy-O, it's me, Clark. Just wanted to make sure that the phone was working properly. We're all in position. Let us know when you're rollin' in. The range on yer device is a quarter mile, so you can just say it out loud in the car. We'll hear ya. Come in from the south and park facing north."

"Oooookay," said Daddy-O as he hung up the phone. "We on fellas."

MICHAEL LEE

EIGHTEEN

SURPRISINGLY, SKATELAND'S parking lot was on jam. They were five minutes early. It was kind of chilly out, so most of the patrons were inside. The sloppy, out of shape security guard stood inside the glass front door. As Denard navigated through the crowded parking lot, looking for an empty space facing north, Red brought his attention to a black Buick Grand National that was entering the parking lot, as well.

"Dat's dat nigga right dere in dat Grand National," he said. "Park da car. I'm 'bout to go get 'em and bring 'em over here to meet you. Dis shit *shouldn't* take dat long."

Red got out of the car and walked over to the Grand National, which was not yet parked. He leaned in the passenger side window.

"What's up, nigga?" asked Red, as he gave the passenger of the Grand National, Stone, a hand slap.

"Your world, nigga. Homeboy in that car over there?" inquired Stone.

"Yeah, man. He da one dat's drivin'."

CHANDLER PARK DRIVE

"How you know this nigga? And how you know he ain't 5-0?"

"C'mon, man. I ain't never turnt you on to no shaky jake ass niggas before. He scraight. I done already peeped his game. Nigga got fat bank from his dead rich ass daddy in Southfield. Nigga jus' wanna make a name fo' his self out dere in Oakland County."

"Alright. I hope, for yo' sake, he cool. Here," as Stone handed Red a coin envelope, "give this to that nigga."

"He wanna meet you, man. I told 'em I could put 'em down wit' you. You fuckin' wit' my cut now, nigga. Dis muhhfucker wouldn't even've came out if he didn't think he was gon' meet you."

"Yeah, Red, alright. Tell that nigga to get out the car and meet me. I don't need to see that other nigga."

Stone got out of the car, as Red sprinted back to Denard. Stone was about 25 or 30 years old. He was dark-skinned, about 6'2", 225 lbs. Chiseled. He was sporting a high-top fade, with an S-Curl. His thin moustache had a scar going through it on the left side. He was wearing some black Guess Jeans, black Mauri gators, black mock turtle neck and a rust Marc Buchanan waist length shearling.

Red gave Denard the package and Denard gave him the $150. Red told Denard Stone's conditions. Denard got out of the car and approached Stone on foot. Jason, who remained in the car, apprised the listening crews of what was happening. Slyly, Red passed the money to Stone before making the introduction and excusing himself back to the UCV.

"Yeah, Stone dis Daddy-O."

"You can call me Big 'O', man. That Daddy-O shit is for my hoes," remarked Denard. He seemed to have broken the ice nicely, as Stone cracked a half-assed smile.

"Dig that. Name's Stone, man."

Right at that point, an airplane passed overhead. The sound of its engine's low roar captured Stone's attention, as he looked upward. Denard then realized that the plane was part of his operation. He quickly tried to divert Stone's attention away from the plane back to the matter at hand.

"Like I told your man," started Denard, "I'll be back to holler at you again if them cookies taste anything like mama used to make. Can I give you my beeper number? Or can I get your number? I don't like havin' to go through Red for everything. Ya know what I'm sayin'?"

"Yeah, I know how it is. I can give you my beeper number. Fuck it. If I don't wanna talk to you, I just won't call you back. Let me get your beeper number, too. If I call you, I'm gonna put my code in. It's 292."

They exchanged numbers, got back into their respective vehicles and drove away.

Not even a minute had passed when the cellular phone rang in the car. Denard answered.

"Hello," he said.

"So how did it go? This is Clark."

"The deal is down, baby!" an excited Denard replied.

CHANDLER PARK DRIVE

"Alright. We're gonna stay put right here for another fifteen minutes or so just in case their doin' some counter-surveillance. Y'all go on back to the office. Lefty's on the way back there, too. He'll test the dope for ya. Good job, man."

Daddy-O, Red, Jason, and Lefty met back at the Federal Building. Once back in the office, Red was taken to the CI debriefing room, while the others went into the main office. Lefty took the coin envelope from Daddy-O and began conducting a series of chemical tests on it. Daddy-O scurried to the bathroom. His stomach ache had gotten the better of him, but he rejoined them in the office relatively quickly, considering.

"Well, it's definitely heroin," said Lefty. "We won't know how pure it is, though, until we send it to our lab in Chicago. They do the qualitative analysis there. He did short you a little bit, though. It was more like eight tenths of a gram. Make sure you say something to him about that the next time you talk to him."

"Really? Why?" inquired Jason.

"That way he'll think you're authentic," replied Lefty. "He might have shorted you intentionally. A real dope dealer is usually so greedy that he's going to complain if he feels he's been cheated out of even a dollar."

"Ohhh, okay," remarked Daddy-O. "I got you."

Minutes later, the remainder of the crew showed up. All of Daddy-O's DPD crew members were showing him much love for making his first "big" deal.

Clark, on the other hand, cautioned him about making spur of the moment decisions to change plans, such as getting out of the car to meet Stone. He also reminded the rest of the crew that it wasn't exactly a hand-to-hand buy that they were celebrating. Daddy-O took the critique in the constructive spirit in which he thought it was being given.

The balance of the evening was spent familiarizing the DPD crew with the various reports that have to be completed every time an operation like this concluded. The reports were more lengthy and detailed than the typical DPD report.

As if the night wasn't going well enough for Daddy-O, he got a page from Kathy at about ten-thirty. When he called her back, she told him that she wanted seconds. Still riding high on his adrenaline rush, Daddy-O accepted the invitation.

In what would become an, almost, nightly ritual, and exactly one hour after he had talked to her on the telephone, Daddy-O was the recipient of a Kathy London blowjob. She licked the head of his boner for, what seemed like, an eternity. Then she stroked it with her hand, while licking his balls at the same time. He just lied on his back with his eyes closed, grabbing sheets and licking his bottom lip.

Once she felt that he had reached his maximum potential, she mounted him and rode him like a Ducati until they both exploded. She later saw him to the door before he took that grueling ride home. This time, his conscience really ate away at him. *What was I thinking*, he thought. Clearly this was a big night for him and he

CHANDLER PARK DRIVE

shared his joy with some other woman. On top of all of the guilt, he still had that funny feeling that he was being watched or followed or something, but everything appeared cool as he arrived at home.

MICHAEL LEE

NINETEEN

IN THE MEANTIME, CLARK WAS driving Red to his aunt's house in Highland Park. They were discussing the earlier events.

"So, you thank this guy Daddy-O is gon' be able to find out where Stone has his stash?" asked Clark.

"I think he got a waaayyy better chance dan you and all dem other white boys got."

"I don't know 'bout this guy, Red. It's been five months since you told me about this guy. We done did wiretaps, surveillance and everythang and we still can't figure out where he got his stash. I'm inclined to just go on ahead and hit the Lakewood apartment building."

"Man fuck dat shit. I'm tellin' you what I know, not what I think. Dis nigga 'posed to be done copped like a hun-net birds of boy. I'm tellin' you, I don't know how he foolin' y'all, too, but he got dat shit stashed somewhere. I'll bet his foot soldiers don't even know where it's at. I figger if y'all get a nigga to spend some real loot wit his ass, we can figger it out. You *know* I want y'all to pop dat nigga more dan anybody.

CHANDLER PARK DRIVE

Shit, every time dat nigga get rid of a bird, dat cut into my money."

"You," started Clark, "should have greater concerns about your own well-being. These hand-to-hand buys weren't figured into the original plan. Once we take Stone down, his lawyer is gonna demand that I produce my CI. That, being the case, I can't see your life being worth two red cents afterwards. Plus, even if I *could* put you in the witness protection program, a long trial might prolong our payday."

"Hell, I ain't worried 'bout Stone. Hell, if y'all bust him wit' as much as I think y'all gon' bust 'em wit', he might not even live to go to no trial," laughed Red. "You know how it is. Niggas get smoked everyday for *much* less."

The ride was coming to an end as Clark drove down Pilgrim, off Hamilton. Red jumped out and ran into a large yellow-aluminum sided single family home.

Red and Clark's unique arrangement was born about two years earlier. Red was out with Clark making a buy, when he began discussing his life before he became a snitch. He said that he'd worked for J. L. Hudson's at Eastland Mall in Harper Woods, Michigan. Red told him that he was elevated to Sales Consultant at the Coach display, because of his sense of style. Once he learned the ins and outs of the business, he developed his new con, which ultimately led to his termination, and criminal prosecution.

Red told Clark that he would assist in making the orders for the Coach handbags and accessories. Because he knew exactly what was being ordered, he and his partner, a guy named Snake, from the hood, would then take a trip to New York and buy, almost perfect, replicas of the same items. Once J. L. Hudson's would receive their shipment, he would replace some of the items with the fakes, and personally, sell the fake items to customers that he thought would never notice the difference.

He, then, would sell the authentic items on the street for a fraction of the list price. This turned out to be a lucrative hustle for Red. Months had gone by and nothing happened, until a customer complained to a Customer Service Representative, and the company launched an internal investigation, which revealed Red and his illegal operation.

Red, jokingly, confided to Clark that if he were a police officer, he wouldn't turn in *all* of the dope that he would confiscate. He said that he would take some for himself, and sell it on the street for a fraction of what his competitors were selling it for. The whole notion was, actually, intriguing to Clark. A way to make some extra cash, maybe get his wife to stay at home with the kids, and out of that damned fake foot factory. He found himself pondering over the suggestion, and came up with what he thought was a flawless plan.

Clark rationalized in his mind that he could confiscate drugs and turn all of it in, as required. Understanding the procedure, Clark identified a loophole in the system that would allow someone to

CHANDLER PARK DRIVE

steal drugs and never be detected. It was simple, he thought. Once he confiscated the dope, an analysis would be performed on it to determine if it was, in fact, dope. Subsequent to that first analysis, a second and final analysis would be done to determine the quality of the dope. Barring some extraordinary circumstances, no more analysis would ever be performed on the drugs before they were destroyed. Drugs were made available for destruction soon after the court case concluded.

Clark concluded, in his mind, that he could retrieve analyzed dope from the property room to display during court hearings. Prior to returning the drugs to the property room, he would switch them with packages of identical weight and composition. He'd then take the real drugs and sell them to a buyer for a fraction of the standard street cost. Once he visualized this plan in his mind, he realized that he needed a buyer.

That's where Red came in. A short time later, Clark told Red that he wanted to set up a reverse sting, and to find a dealer with some heavy cash that wanted to buy a kilo or more. Red delivered, introducing Clark as a Biloxi shrimp boater, who frequently had large quantities of drugs to sell from deals he made with Columbians, while sailing the Gulf Coast.

The buyer was this rich white Irish guy named Eddie Malloy that Red met while hanging out at this bar called First Place Lounge on Harper in Detroit. Malloy was a big, burly, young biker type. Red got the impression that he probably despised niggers, but didn't have a problem with taking their money. Red, himself, had bought a few pounds of weed from him. Red figured that he could kill two birds with one stone. First, he could set up the reverse for Clark, and secondly, he could get this racist motherfucker Malloy busted. The introduction and the, subsequent buy went well.

Red, however, got suspicious when he realized that Clark hadn't arrested Malloy after a long time had passed. At one point, even, Clark was *only* interested in popping multi-kilo dealers in open-and-shut type cases, and was angered with Red for bringing him anything but.

Finally, acting on a hunch, Red confronted Clark and told him that he was completely aware of what he was doing and demanded to be cut in or he'd snitch him out. Clark confessed to him that he was selling confiscated drugs to Malloy at wholesale prices. Clark told him about his whole operation, and even confessed that he'd gotten the idea from Red. He said that, to this date, Malloy still doesn't have any idea that he's a fed.

Clark agreed to give Red, in addition to his regular pay, a ten percent sales commission on every seizure that he brought to the table and Clark sold. To date, the hustle had netted over $75,000 for Clark. If the seizure from Stone is large as they both expected, they could both be very well off, almost overnight.

CHANDLER PARK DRIVE

TWENTY

IT WAS FRIDAY THE THIRTEENTH, and because of that, Daddy-O felt, particularly, uneasy when, at seven-thirty in the evening, his DEA issued pager sounded and the display had a telephone number followed by the numbers, 292, Stone's code. Daddy-O was so shocked by the call that he didn't know what to do. He had already left work for the day. Using what he thought was his best judgment; he contacted Clark by phone to let him know.

"Hello," Clark said.

"Yo, Clark, this is Daddy-O ... Denard."

"Yep, I know. What's goin' on?"

"Stone just paged me, man. He left his code and some strange number in the pager y'all gave me."

"Did you call him first?"

"Naw. I ain't talked to him since the other night."

"That's great. He must've got some good vibes from you. Well, here's what you do. Call him back. Make sure you call him from the cell phone, so's he don't get yer home phone number or nothin'. See what he wants. If he wants to keep dealin' with you, tell him you want to cop an ounce, but you ain't gonna be able to do it 'til tomorrow or Sunday. Just make up a reason. Call me back and let me know how it goes. And, remember, don't worry. You're gonna do just fine."

"Alright. I'll call you back and let you know how it went."

Denard was at home when he'd received the page. Sheila was out. He sat down at his dining room table with the cell phone in his hand. His heart was beating super fast. He took two deep breaths before dialing the number on the cell phone.

"Hello," answered the voice on the other end.

"Speak to Stone," said Denard.

"Who dis?" inquired the male voice.

"This Big O, Daddy-O."

"Oh yeah, what's up Big O ? This Stone, man."

"Hey, what's hat'nin', man?" Denard asked, while trying to sound nonchalant.

"You, nigga. I was jus' wonderin' why I ain't heard from you. That product wasn't straight?"

"Naw, it was the bomb, they tell me."

"So, what, you changed your mind about gettin' a whole pack?"

"Naw, I just figured you ain't want to do no mo' business wit' me," remarked Denard.

"Bullshit. I'm all about bin-ness, baby. What you talkin' 'bout?"

"Well, I figure like this, man. You told me that a cookie was a buck and a half, and I *paid* you a buck and a half."

CHANDLER PARK DRIVE

"And?" asked Stone.

"Then I expect to get a cookie, not half, two-thirds, or three-quarters of a cookie. Now, don't get me wrong, I ain't no twenty-five, thirty dollar mah-fucka, which is all that li'l shortage amounted to, but I'll bet you wouldn't've wanted your *money* to be short by that much. So, anyway, I just figured, to avoid any confusion in the future, I'll just nip this shit in the bud and take my business elsewhere."

"Look, man. I ain't no twenty-five or thirty dollar nigga, either, and I ain't gon' let no twenty-five or thirty dollars stop us from doin' bin-ness. If you say it was short, I'll take your word for it. I don't weigh that shit personally. I got niggas that work for me that do that shit, but I'm glad you let me know 'cause now I can handle *my* bin-ness. But as far as that little shortage go, we can take care of that shit on the next deal."

"*That's* what I'm talkin' about; customer satisfaction. Well, dig dis here. I still wanna cop that whole pack, but I'll have to get back wit' you tomorrow or Sunday. I'm supposed to be takin' my kids to the drive-in tonight. You know how it is, I gotta do that daddy thang."

"Okay. Well, just call me tomorrow or the next day, or whatever and we can hook it up. What size package you think you gon' want?"

"'Bout a onion size."

"Alright. Let me know, so I can put it together. And dig dis here, from now on, leave dat nigga Red outta my and your bin-ness, and let's keep this shit one-on-one from here on out, dog."

"Cool. I'll holler at you later."

"Peace out."

Denard hung up the cell phone and started jumping up and down, doing the Cabbage Patch and the Running Man. He couldn't believe that he had pulled it off. He could hardly contain himself, as he called Clark back to report on what had just occurred.

"Hello," said Clark.

"It's on, baby!"

"What?"

"I told him that I would get back to him either tomorrow or Sunday and that I wanted to buy an ounce from him. He was, like, all in."

"How much did he say that he'd sell you an ounce for?" inquired Clark.

"Damn. I forgot to ask him how much it was gonna cost? Well, I figure we can talk about that when I call him back."

"Okay. Sounds good. Where does he want to do the deal."

"To be honest with you, man, we didn't go into any of the details other than I want to buy it and that he would sell it to me. I was just trying to get the right conversation from him and then hurry up and get off the phone before he changed his mind or somethin'. Hell, I don't know, man. I'll try to be a lot more thorough, though, the next time I talk to him."

"No problem. Just one last thang. Make some real good notes about this phone call, including the time it occurred, 'cause you're gon' have to do a report when you get to the office. I'll let you know whether we're gon' do this deal on Saturday or Sunday. Is your crew off duty on both days?"

"Yeah, we are," said Denard. "We just worked last weekend, but I'm sure that Slickster can work somethin' out for us on this."

"Alright. I'll give Slickster a call and talk to you later. Good job."

"Thanks."

Denard grabbed his home phone and commenced calling. His first call was to Jason. He, jubilantly, shared the news of his triumphant telephone conversation. Jason was elated and looked forward to doing the deal. His next call was to Sheila on her cell phone. She said that she was happy for him, but seemed preoccupied with the manicure that she said she was getting. Finally, he called Kathy. Pay dirt.

MICHAEL LEE

TWENTY-ONE

NOON SUNDAY, EVERYONE FROM both the DEA and the DPD crews met at the DEA Office in the Federal Building. The deal was set to go down today. It was just a matter of contacting Stone and agreeing on a time and a location. Although, the price had not yet been established, Fordham had $10,000 cash on hand, which should have been more than enough to buy an ounce of heroin. Clark, Slickster, and Daddy-O went into the interrogation room to drop the dime on Stone. Clark recorded the conversation.

"Remember what I told you, Daddy-O," started Clark. "Try to give us at least a couple of hours so that we can get in place."

"Alright," said a nervous Denard.

"And don't forget. You need to know the price which, by the way, should be somewhere around five thousand to seventy-five hundred, depending on the quality of his stuff. If he goes any higher than that, then haggle with him. He'll know that if you pay more than that for an ounce, then you *got* to be the police. Okay. You ready?"

CHANDLER PARK DRIVE

"As ready as I'll ever be." Denard raised his eyebrows and looked at Slickster, who was seated across the table from him with his left elbow on top of it. His chin was cuffed in his left hand. The fingers were slowly stroking his beard. Clark started the recorder as Denard began to dial.

"Hello," said Stone.

"Hey, what's up, man? This Big O."

"My man! What's up, baby? What you need?"

"Yeah, man, I wanna see about gettin' one of them onions, today."

"Oh, okay," replied Stone, as though he was pondering something. "I can do that, man, but it's gon' cost you sixty-four. I normally charge sixty-five, but since we got off to such a bad start, I'm givin' you a discount. But that's a one time only deal, though."

"Damn, man, sixty-five seem kinda like on the high end, man."

"Yeah, it's a little bit up there, but you ain't gon' find nuttin' no more pure than my shit out there. Hey, you welcome to look."

"Naw, my peoples say your shit is tight, so uhh, let's do this."

"Well, I got it right now. All you got to do is come by my joint on the east side. You know where Lakewood is?"

"Yeah. Ain't that like right near Chalmers?"

"Yeah. One street over. I'm in the apartment building on the corner of Charlevoix. You can come to apartment 308, and I'll serve you up. You can even weigh it then."

"All due respect, man. I ain't comin' up in no joint. That's all I need is for the police to come runnin' up in there while I'm there. Why don't you, uhh, just bring it out to my car, man? I'll be in that same Taurus I was in the other day."

"Damn, don't tell me you one of them ol' suburbanite muh-fuckas, scared of niggas in the city."

"If that was the case, I wouldn't be doin' no business wit' you. I just don't like goin' up in joints period. No matter what city they in."

"Cool your horses, nigga. I'll bring it out to you. Just hit me up on the cell phone when you here. 'Bout what time you comin'?"

"It's gon' take me a couple minutes to get this cheddar together, but I should be there between two and three."

"Alright. I'll see you then ... Come by yo' self, nigga."

"I know. I know. See ya later." Denard hung up the phone.

Clark rewound the tape and the three of them listened. When it ended, Slickster and Clark slapped Denard five. They went back to the main office for the briefing.

Knowing that it was probably goin' down today, Denard dressed for the part. He was wearing his Timberland boots, Used jeans, a 'Bill Cosby' type sweater, black skully, and a Marc Buchanan leather jacket.

"Okay guys," started Clark, "The call went well. Daddy-O set up a deal that is s'posed to go down

CHANDLER PARK DRIVE

between two and three. It's twelve-thirty now, so that still gives us a couple hours to set up. The only problem I see is that Stone wants to do the deal on Lakewood. Now, we all know that that place is s'posed to be wired for games, so we ain't gon' be able to position ourselves as close as the last time. Slickster, you think you and your people can go out and try to identify where they got their counter-surveillance people?"

"Sure, that won't be a problem," replied Slickster.

"Great. Uhh, we'll be guided by you as to where we need to position ourselves. I'll get the bird in the air, too."

"Wait a minute," began Denard. "I don't think I want that airplane up. The last time, he looked up at it as it flew by. I think he's gonna be a little bit suspicious if every time I come around, there's a plane flying by. I would just rather you didn't use it if you don't have to."

"No," said Clark. "We don't *have* to use it, but it's nice to have. But if it makes you feel more comfortable without it, then we won't use it."

"Thanks," responded Daddy-O.

"Just one more thang," remarked Clark. "Because we're spendin' so much money this time, you're gon' have to get the field analysis done quicker, so Lefty is gon' meet up with you somewhere right after the buy."

"Alright," said Daddy-O.

Everyone received their assignments, Daddy-O got his toys and money, and they all set out on the street. It was about two-thirty when Clark called

Daddy-O on the phone and told him that everything was a go. Daddy-O was in the process of drinking a Coke that he'd gotten from the McDonald's drive-thru on Mack and Conner. He was hoping that it would help settle his nerve induced stomach ache. He started rolling toward the target location.

Once he parked outside of the location, he called Stone on the phone. Stone told him that he'd be right out. Red was right about the Lakewood apartment, he thought. Everywhere he looked, he saw shady looking characters on the street corners, and looking out the windows. He seemed to be the focus of everyone's attention. He just tried to look natural and remain calm.

Even though it was only about 40° outside, Stone came out of the building wearing only a sweatshirt with the words Treat 'Em Right on the front, some Adidas track pants, a doo rag on his head, and a pair of Air Jordans; unlaced. He got into the car from the passenger side, and pulled a clear plastic bag containing the tan colored substance from his pants pocket; almost in one fluid motion. He passed the package to Daddy-O.

"Here you go. Go on and weigh it if you want to. Test it. Whatever you gotta do."

Daddy-O examined the package in a discriminating fashion, before rendering his verdict.

"Naw, I don't need to weigh it right now. I know where you at. If it's anything wrong with it, I'll get back wit' you." He then gave Stone the money and told him to count it.

CHANDLER PARK DRIVE

Stone thumbed through the first nine or ten hundred dollar bills, as though he was counting it. He rolled it all back up into a wad and jammed it into his pocket.

"Okay, dog," said Stone as he offered Daddy-O some dap. "It look straight. Let me know if you wanna do sump'n else." Not even waiting for a response from Daddy-O, he got out of the car and trotted up to and back into the apartment building.

Denard, now extremely bothered by his upset stomach, sped away. Almost immediately, Denard had that funny feeling again like he was being watched or followed or something. About two blocks away from the apartment building, he noticed a car following behind him. Paranoid, and concerned that some of Stone's goons were trailing him, he turned onto the first street he came to, and so did the car. He then turned at the next corner and started speeding, the car continued to follow.

Suddenly the cell phone rang.

"Hello!" yelled Denard.

"What's going on?" asked Clark.

"It's some motherfucker following me! I'm trying to lose him!"

"Whoa," said Clark. "We were wondering what you were doing. That's Lefty behind you."

Feeling stupid, Denard slapped his forehead and said, "Oh shit. I forgot about him."

"Yeah," said Clark. "Y'all need to stop and get that dope analyzed."

"Okay," a relieved Denard responded.

MICHAEL LEE

Denard drove to Jackson Middle School's parking lot. Lefty tested the package, and sure enough, it was dope. Denard could hardly wait to get back to the Federal building so that he could race to the nearest bathroom. As much as he had hoped to, he couldn't escape the ridicule that everyone gave him for running from Lefty. He was the brunt of every joke as they completed the paperwork.

Later that evening, Denard got together with his whole crew and went to the 411 Bar down the street from Police Headquarters downtown to celebrate him busting his one ounce cherry over some cheap drinks. Sheila joined the party. They closed the bar. Slickster gave the crew the next day off, since they worked on their leave day.

CHANDLER PARK DRIVE

TWENTY-TWO

DENARD ONLY HAD ONE WEEK TO bask in the glory of his first big deal. It was only eight days later, on a Monday, three days before Thanksgiving, that the crews met at the Federal Building for, what would be their final gathering until the following Monday, after the holiday. Clark had devised a plan that he'd seen work in the past, and shared it with the crew.

"I want us to try to get a buy out of Stone again today," said Clark. "I thank that this is the perfect time, since a lot of folks are goin' on vacation and all. Daddy-O can tell 'em that he sold out of his last pack, and he just wanna re-up for the holiday."

"That's believable," added Daddy-O. "Cats be re-uppin' for the holidays all the time."

"Yeah," stated Clark, "But there's just one catch. You're gon' tell 'em that you want to re-up and that you want another pack, but once you meet with 'em, tell 'em that you want two ounces. This way we catch him off balance. Either he's gon' have it on him or he ain't. If he doesn't, then he's either gon' have to decide to go get it or let the sale go. Ideally, if he's sittin' there lookin' at twice as much money as he thought he was gon' get, the greed factor gon' kick in. If it does, then we'll try to follow him and find out where he goes to get his stuff."

"That's a damn good idea," remarked Slickster.

"It's a good idea if he takes the bait," said a skeptical Jason.

"Well, I ain't gon' say it's a full proof plan," cautioned Clark, "But I *have* seen it work in other cases. And if it fails, hey, at least we got another buy into 'em."

Daddy-O dropped a dime on Stone at approximately the same time of day that he called him the week prior. Stone went along with doing the deal, but he told Daddy-O that he wouldn't be available until later that evening; around six o'clock. Daddy-O agreed to meet him at the Lakewood apartment at six.

Daddy-O spent most of the day tinkering around the DEA office, kickin' it with the guys on the crew. He noticed booklets lying around the office entitled U.S. Justice Department Intelligence Reports. As he thumbed through the reports, he noticed one article that identified the only regions of the world that cocaine can be grown and manufactured. None of the regions were in the United States. Another article indicated that the penalty for possessing crack cocaine was twice as harsh for possessing the same amount of powder cocaine. He wondered if the fact that blacks were more likely to possess crack had anything to do with it.

CHANDLER PARK DRIVE

The information contained in the reports prompted him to contemplate why the U.S. government, with its vast resources, wasn't waging the drug war at the source instead of in America. He didn't want to believe it, but his brother Earl, a self-proclaimed conspiracy theorist, had told him on many times before that there was no war on drugs, but a war on black men in America selling drugs.

By the time four o'clock rolled around, everyone was in place. Denard listened to their chatter from a radio in the office. They were describing light to medium traffic at the location, as well as a lot of counter-surveillance activity. It seemed like the two hours came and went in a flash.

"I'm rollin' in," Denard said aloud once he was two blocks away from Lakewood. Once he pulled up, he called Stone on the phone to let him know that he was there. Stone told him that he'd be right out. Stone came out of the building, stood on the corner, and looked around for a whole minute before getting into the car.

"You alright, man?" asked Daddy-O.

"I'm straight. Just one of my boys told me he seen 5-0 parked around the block earlier. He say he went back about a half hour ago and they was gone, though."

"I know you ain't tryin' to say that I'm 5-0."

"I ain't tryin' to say shit. You tryin' to say it?"

"Man, far as I know, you the motherfuckin' police, but the bottom line is, I done already copped from you, so if you gonna arrest me, go on ahead."

"I tell you what, if you are 5-0, you done fooled the shit outta me. Anyway, let's do bin-ness, dog. Here." Stone hurled an ounce bag of heroin into Daddy-O's lap.

"Aww, my bad, dog," said Daddy-O, as he pulled the much-larger-than-the-last-time wad of money from his jacket pocket. "I forgot to tell you. I want to cop two O's this time."

Stone's eyes seemed to get a little bigger as he spied the cash in Daddy-O's hand.

"Damn. I wish you woulda told me that when you called earlier."

"Fuck it. If you ain't got it, I'll just take the one. I was tryin' to load up for the holiday."

"Hold on. Just wait right here. I'll be back." Stone took the dope, got out of the car, and re-entered the apartment building. Five minutes later he returned.

"Check this out, dog, I need you to run me somewhere right quick."

"I ain't got all day, man. Where we goin'?"

"I'm tryin' to get you these two O's. You want 'em, don't you."

"Yeah, alright. Where we goin'?"

"Just drive. I'll tell you how to get there."

"I mean, tell me somethin', man. Is it in Detroit, or what?"

"Yeah. It's in Detroit. It ain't far from here. Just drive."

CHANDLER PARK DRIVE

Stone directed Daddy-O to drive north on Conner and make a right on Chandler Park Drive. Daddy-O was hopeful that someone from his crew was following. He did notice a pair of headlights behind him that followed him into the park. However, once he had driven the entire distance of the winding and twisting park, and past the golf course, which was uninhabited, Stone told him to make a u-turn and go back.

"What? You don't know where in the hell you goin'?" inquired Daddy-O.

"Nigga, wise up. How else you gon' make sure the police ain't followin' you?"

Daddy-O realized then that Stone's crafty maneuver through Chandler Park Drive might have worked; much to his chagrin. Two minutes later, as he proceeded north on Conner, the cell phone rang. The first thought that popped into Daddy-O's mind was Clark telling him that if he calls on that phone, something's wrong. Daddy-O tried to look normal as possible as he answered.

"Hello," he said.

"Is everything alright?" asked Clark.

"Oh yeah, I'm straight, dog. I'm in the middle of some business right now but I can call you back."

"I just wanted to let you know that you're outside of our listening range and we lost you on the tail when he went through Chandler Park."

"Yeah, I know, but check this out, I'm in the middle of somethin' right now," responded Daddy-O. He, then, hung up the phone. "Motherfuckers act like they don't understand when you say you busy, you busy."

"I heard that," replied Stone. "Alright, now slow down. Turn right on Six Mile. ... Okay now, pull over riiight here."

Stone got out of the car and walked over to a small storefront building that appeared to be vacant. He unlocked the security grate on the front door and went inside. He came out three minutes later, locked the building up, and got back in the car.

"You in luck, nigga," said Stone as he tossed two one ounce bags to Daddy-O. "That was the last ounce I could scrape up. I need to re-up my damn self. I'm low than a motherfucker."

Daddy-O gave him the money and they rode back to Lakewood, while bouncin' to Heavy D's We Got Our Own Thang, on WJLB. After Daddy-O dropped Stone off, he noticed that he didn't have a stomach ache, and couldn't remember whether he'd had one at all during this deal. He couldn't wait to get out of the area and call the crew.

"Hello," answered Clark.

"Where we gon' meet up to test this dope?"

"You got it?"

"Hell yeah, two packs. What's my name?"

"Great! We'll meet you at Angel Park. You know where that is?"

"Yep. I'm on the way."

Everyone met up at the park. It was as though they were gonna do a pre-raid briefing. Daddy-O jumped out of the UCV and hastened to Lefty's car.

CHANDLER PARK DRIVE

Lefty had the dome light on in his car and the test kits ready. Daddy-O jumped in and handed the packages over to Lefty.

"So, it went pretty good, huh?" asked Lefty.

"Aww, man," began Daddy-O. "That shit was kinda scary there for a minute. I mean …," at that point Jason had joined them and he got into the backseat. "I figured that when we went through Chandler Park, that he was tryin' to clean his self, but when Clark called me and told me that it had worked, I was like, DAMN!"

"Yeah, man. I was scared for you," said Jason. "I *know* how you feel about it, but that plane would have come in handy today. Do you realize that we had no contact whatsoever with you for twenty minutes almost?"

"Damn. It didn't seem like it was that long."

"It's dope," said Lefty.

By now, Clark and Slickster have walked over to Lefty's car. Daddy-O and Jason got out to talk to them.

"The deal is down, baby," said Daddy-O, as he embraced Slickster.

"Good job," said Slickster.

"So, where did y'all go?" asked Clark.

"We went to this, looked like it was abandoned, storefront building on Six Mile, off Conner. I didn't get the address, but I can take you by there if you wanna see."

"Is that where his stash is at?" asked Clark.

"I really can't say. I wanna say it is, but after he came out, he told me that I had copped his last ounce and that he had to re-up."

MICHAEL LEE

Clark had heard all that he needed, because he knew that Stone had fed Daddy-O a line of bullshit, trying to throw him off the scent, while stroking his ego at the same time. Daddy-O took Clark to the building to get the address. They all departed from the park and met at the office for the dreaded paperwork.

When Clark left the office for the day, he telephoned Red from his personal cell phone.

"You ain't gon' believe what happened today," said Clark.

"What? Stone dropped dead and left a roadmap to his dope?"

"No, you stupid motherfucker. Even better. He took Daddy-O to his stash spot."

"Well, I'll be damned. Dat nigga Daddy-O badder dan I thought he was. Dat was quick dan a muhfucka."

"Anyway, I don't plan on wasting too much more time on this case. I should be makin' a move on it real soon."

"Alright, man. Thanks for da call. I'll talk to ya later." They hung up.

Clark placed another call.

"Hello," answered the female voice.

"Is Eddie home?" asked Clark.

"Hold on," she said. "Who should I tell him is callin'?"

"Tell him it's Biloxi Bob."

"Hello."

"How's it goin', Eddie?"

CHANDLER PARK DRIVE

"Well, I'm fair for a square. You know how it is."

"I got somethin' for you."

"What you got?"

"I don't know if you can handle this one."

"Believe me, me and my boys can handle anything you got."

"Speakin' of boys; you think you can take anywhere from, say, forty to seventy-five of 'em off my hands for about a dime apiece?"

"That *is* a lot. How hot is *this* shit?"

"At a dime apiece, what do you care?"

"Alright. I'll tell you what. Don't talk to nobody else yet. Call me tomorrow and I'll let you know. Okay?"

"Talk to you tomorrow."

MICHAEL LEE

TWENTY-THREE

THANKSGIVING. THE BLAKE CLAN had gathered at Denard's parents' house. It was about four o'clock. The men of the family, which included Blake, his brothers Earl, and Martin, father Daniel, brother-in-law, Kenneth, and nephew, Martin, Jr., were in the den lamenting the end of the Lions-Oilers game. The game clock was winding down, and Barry Sanders had put on only a lackluster 54-yard performance in the losing effort. The women, Vency, Denard's mom, Sheila, sister-in-law, Danita, his sisters Karen, and Audrey, were putting the finishing touches on dinner in the kitchen. All of Denard's five nieces were playing with baby dolls and stuff in the basement.

Vency came into the den and announced that dinner was served, and asked everyone into the dining room. She wanted Martin, the preacher in the family, to bless the food while everyone joined hands in a circle.

"Let us bow our heads," said Martin. "Father, we want to thank you once again for this opportunity for family to fellowship together. We thank you for all that is seen and unseen, Father. We thank you for the many

CHANDLER PARK DRIVE

blessings that you have bestowed on this family, Lord. We ask that you touch every heart here and bless 'em, Lord, according to their individual needs, God. Lord, bless the food that has been prepared here today, Lord. Bless those that took part in its preparation, and bless those that will consume it, Lord. Lord, let it be nourishment for our bodies, Lord, that it may strengthen us to be healthier and stronger Christians, Lord. For these, and other blessings I ask, in Jesus name. Amen."

"Amen," said the family.

After the women were allowed to prepare the younger children's plates first, the adults partook of the roasted turkey, cornbread dressing, giblet gravy, turnip greens, macaroni and cheese, yams, string beans, potato salad, dinner rolls and cranberry sauce, while engaging in casual conversation at the dinner table, and kitchen table. The kids ate in grandma's bedroom and in the basement.

"So, what's happ'nin' with the police department, Denny?" asked Earl.

"You know much as I do," said Denard; not wanting to engage his brother in another conspiracy debate.

"You still workin' the narcotics?" he asked.

"Yeah. As a matter of fact, I'm assigned out to the DEA, now."

"The DEA!" exclaimed his youngest sister, Audrey. "Isn't that even more dangerous than what you were doing before?"

"I tried to tell 'em girl," said Sheila. "You ought to know, you can't tell yo' brother nothing."

"Like I told Sheila. This is somethin' that I always wanted to do. I don't think it's no more dangerous than anything else. Think about it. How often do you here about a narcotics officer getting killed? Almost never. Patrol is the most dangerous job out there."

Denard's father Daniel had removed his false teeth to eat, but joined in the conversation, without hesitation. "I know what you mean, though, Denny. When y'all go up and bust them houses, y'all be ready! Y'all don't be takin' no stuff! They just don't be that kind of prepared in them patrol cars. Hey, since Clinton won the election, what you think he gon' do for the city? I know Coleman Young got to be glad them Republicans are out of office."

"Yeah, Denny," chimed Martin. "I've been meaning to ask you about that. Do you think Clinton is gonna be good for law enforcement, in general?"

"Well, I think so. Plus, I think he's gonna hook *us* up big time. The city, that is. Coleman was pretty instrumental in gettin' him elected."

In an effort to change the subject, Vency interjected. "Hmmm, hmmm, hmmm, hmm, hmm, this macaroni and cheese is outta sight, Sheila. What did you do to get it so creamy?"

"Mom, I just watched you. I probably couldn't make it that good again, if I tried."

Denard's pager went off. It was Jason. He excused himself from the table to return the call.

"Hello," said Jason.

"Yo, what's up, dog?"

CHANDLER PARK DRIVE

"Did you hear what happened last night?"

"Naw. What?"

"Your boy Stone got smoked at the Climax II."

"He what?!!!!"

"You heard me. Some motherfucker cancelled his damn contract last night."

"Goddd-DAMN!" exclaimed Denard. "How you find out?"

"My boy at Homicide. He works Special Assignment Squad. He always calls me whenever some dope boy gets smoked, 'cause they handle all of those types of cases. He just called me to see if I knew anything about him. I told him we was workin' him, but I didn't tell him anything else."

"So, who shot him?" asked Denard.

"I don't know. He said it was a drive by. Basically, what I got from him was that he was comin' out of the club at about two o'clock when it was closin' and some guy wearin' a ski mask in an old black caddie pulled up and shot him three times. Witnesses say Stone tried to get his shit out and fire back. They did find his gun lying right next to his body. Oh yeah, and my boy did say that the feebies came over to Homicide and looked at the file, too."

"The feebies?"

"Yeah, the feebies," said Jason. "Oh yeah, my bad. I forgot you was kinda on the square side. That's the F.B.I., fool."

"Why they lookin' at it?"

"He didn't say. But man, it could be anything. Stone *was* getting' dollars like that, you know."

"Damn," said Denard, while shaking his head in disbelief. "Uhhn, uhhn, uhn. Oh well," he sighed. "There goes my court case."

"Hey, man," started Jason. "Where you at? I called your house, but didn't get an answer."

"I'm over my mother and father's house. We're having Thanksgiving dinner over here."

"Oh, okay. Tell your parents I said hello. Did you see that ol' fucked up football game? They need to fire Wayne Fontes' ass, don't they?"

"Hell yeah. But, hey man, listen. I gotta go. When you called, I was sittin' down eatin'. Let me get back to my plate before my food gets cold."

"Alright. If I don't talk to you before then, I'll see you Monday."

"Later. Oh, and Happy Thanksgiving to you and yours, too, man."

"Thanks, man. I'll talk to you later."

Denard and Sheila finished dinner, helped with the dishes, and departed for home. The ride home was conversation-filled.

"Well, you may have gotten your wish," said Denard.

"What are you talking about?" asked Sheila.

"You know the case that I've been workin' with the feds?"

"Yeah. You're the undercover on it, right?"

"Yeah. Well, anyway, the guy that I've been makin' the buys from got killed last night."

CHANDLER PARK DRIVE

"Oh my God. What happened?"

"Jason called me and told me. I guess somebody did a drive by on him at the Climax II, last night."

"I *hate* that club," remarked Sheila. "It seems like somebody's always getting shot or something, there. I hate to hear that somebody that you were working got killed, but how does that affect your case?"

"Good question. I don't think we can dig him up and charge him with delivery or nothin'," he said, jokingly. "So I guess the case will be considered closed. I'm just speculatin', though. Ain't no tellin' what direction the feds are gonna go with this. I haven't talked to anyone from over there yet. They're probably more upset about it than I am. All that money and time gone to waste."

"Well, like I said, I'm sorry to hear about this guy, but as far as I'm concerned, it was better him than you."

"You know what?" began Denard. "I kinda had a feelin' somethin' like this was gon' happen."

"How so?"

"Well, lately, and I ain't talkin' about the other night when they was ridin' me at the bar for runnin' from Lefty, but lately I've had this really weird feelin' that somebody's been watchin' me or followin' me or somethin'. I don't know. Maybe I've just been paranoid since I started making these buys for the feds."

"Well, maybe you can relax now since the case is closed."

"Yeah. Maybe."

TWENTY-FOUR

MONDAY, WHEN DADDY-O ARRIVED at the Federal Building, everyone seemed to be moving at warp speed. They were loading raid vans and suiting up.

"What's goin' on?" Denard asked Too Sweet, as he passed by.

"Fordham says that we're gonna hit two of Stone's spots today," Too Sweet replied. "You did hear about what happened to Stone over the weekend, didn't you?"

"Yeah. Jason called and told me."

"Well, hey look, man. You need to start getting' suited up. Slick said that they wanna be rollin' in the next fifteen or twenty minutes."

"Okay. Let me grab my shit."

The briefing took place in the parking lot across the street from the Federal Building. It was decided that both crews would raid the Lakewood apartment building together, considering all of the challenges that it presented. It was further decided that the DEA crew would then go to the Six Mile location after Lakewood

CHANDLER PARK DRIVE

had been secured. After the briefing concluded, they loaded into their respective raid vans. The segregation provided each crew the opportunity to discuss what they didn't want to say in front of each other.

"Slick, who decided, and when, that we were gonna hit these two joints?" asked Daddy-O.

"Well, I guess Clark talked to Fordham and let him know that his CI thinks that Stone's people are scrambling, trying to get rid of Stone's dope. Plus, with no one knowing who killed Stone, they are hoping to stumble across some leads like this. It could've been an *inside* job, you know. Wouldn't be the first time that one of these, so-called kingpins' underlings took 'em out."

"Yeah, I understand all of that," said Daddy-O. "I just wish that *I* would've been included in the decision-making process. I mean, think about it, we wouldn't even know anything about the Six Mile spot if it wasn't for me, and we ain't even gon' get to hit it with 'em."

"That is kinda fucked up, Slick," said Pounder. "I knew they were gonna figure out a way to squeeze us out."

"C'mon now guys, let's put this into perspective. We wouldn't be hittin' neither one of these joints right now if Stone wouldn't have went and got his self killed," remarked F.A.

"Exactly," said Slickster. "Let's just see what happens. Who knows? The mother lode might be on Lakewood."

"I hope so," said Daddy-O. "I think Stone wasn't lying when he said he was out. That'll serve 'em right if they get over there and it's a dry hole."

The tone in the DEA van was slightly different.

"I hope this doesn't turn out to be a dry run," said Prowler. "Hell, it's been four days since they killed this guy. I'm sure that *somebody* in his organization was smart enough to get rid of, or at least move, the dope by now."

"Prowler," began Clark, "I'll bet you dinner at the Outback, *including dranks,* that we find the mother lode."

"You're on, buddy," said Prowler.

"Can I get a piece of that action too, Clark?" inquired Lefty.

"Sure. Why not? I'm gon' win this one anyway. My CI is certain that this guy is on full. I don't care what he told Daddy-O. I thank that was just a line of bullshit anyways to throw Daddy-O off the scent." He spat some tobacco.

"Well, I hope you're right, you nasty fucker," said Prowler. "It'll be worth the price of a dinner to get a major pop. Be even nicer if we get a body to go with it."

The assault on the Lakewood building was violent, yet systematic. Lookouts were whistling the minute the vans turned onto Charlevoix. Patrol officers detained two crack heads in the back yard after they jumped from second story windows. It took less than 45 seconds to breach the heavily fortified front door. The assault on apartment 308 was swift and deliberate.

CHANDLER PARK DRIVE

The only people inside of apartment 308 were Stone's girlfriend, Tamika and their 4-year old son. The apartment was lavish, by ghetto standards. Gawdy Italian leather furniture, a 60" projection TV, velvet art, and plenty of dirty, yet expensive, clothes lying about was the decorum. The officers felt that they had hit pay dirt when they located a half-kilo of heroin in the master bedroom. The half-kilo was broken down into ounces. The seventeen packages were each stuffed in the toe of seventeen different shoes.

"Oooh, baby!" shouted Daddy-O. "We hit a lick up in this motherfucker." He, quickly, placed his hand over his mouth, remembering that there was a 4-year old present. "I mean, this was a nice hit."

"Yeah, this was great, Daddy-O," said Clark. "Is this apartment in your name, ma'am?"

"I pay the rent here," Tamika replied.

"C'mon lady, that is an easy to answer question," said Slickster, obviously frustrated. "Are you the person who this apartment is rented to?"

"Oh, oh, yes, I'm sorry. I didn't understand what he was sayin."

"Thank you," replied Slickster. "F.A., see if you can find some proof of residency with her name on it."

"I'm already on top of it, boss," F.A. replied.

"Serge," started Clark. "We were about to ..."

"You guys, go ahead," interrupted Slickster. "We can handle the rest here. We'll be taking her in to the Fifth Precinct as soon as we can find a relative to take this kid."

"Alright," responded Clark. "We'll hit you on the air and let you know how we did over there."

"No problem," said Slickster. "And you guys be careful."

"What do we have here?" said Pounder, capturing everyone's attention as he exited the master bedroom, carrying an AK-47 assault rifle.

Tamika began to sob, saying "That's not mine. It's not mine. That belonged to my boyfriend."

"No. *You* guys be careful," said Lefty, as the DEA crew left the building.

Less than ten minutes later, the DEA was breaching the door of the Six Mile location. The building was larger inside than it looked from the outside. It appeared to be an old candy store turned flop house. The place was filthy. Rat droppings littered the floors and countertops. The stench of standing urine and feces in a non-working commode was strong. Nothing about this place was inviting; by anyone's standards. The big break came when Lefty shouted from a rear room, "C'mere fellas!"

Lefty had lifted up what appeared to be a trapped door underneath an old dirty rug. The space, which was about six feet long, four feet wide, and eighteen inches deep, contained brick on top of brick of packaged heroin, and a small satchel full of money. Clark quickly got on his cell phone and summoned Fordham to the scene. Lefty contacted Slickster and crew via radio and told them that they'd hit the mother lode, although there were no people on the premises.

CHANDLER PARK DRIVE

When Fordham arrived, the crew was seated in the building with the door wide open to air it out, counting money and processing evidence.

"How much money was there, Clark?" inquired Fordham.

"We're countin' it fer a second time, boss, but we came up with a hundred and seventy-four thousand dollars," replied Clark. "There's thirty-nine kilos of heroin. Lefty's field-testing each package. We're handlin' everythang as careful as we can so's we can have it dusted fer prints later."

"Nobody was here?" asked Fordham.

"No sir," said Clark. "Nobody here but us mice."

"How did we do at the Lakewood location?"

"Oh, yeah. Slickster and his crew should be wrappin' thangs up over there. They had an arrest. Stone's girlfriend. I thank we got about a half a kilo over there and an AK-47."

"Did you contact the media yet?"

"No sir," responded Clark. "I thought I'd leave that up to the big wigs like you. I figured that you might want to hold a press conference on this tomorrow, though. Lefty and I will volunteer to run it over to the lab tonight, have them test it overnight, and have it back here before the twelve o'clock news. That way, since we didn't get no arrest, we can boast on how pure it is, and believe me when I tell you that this stuff is *good*."

"That's not a bad idea. Alright, you guys go ahead. Make sure you get some rest tonight. And NO drinking."

Slickster and his crew, with the exception of F.A. and Pounder, who were busy at the precinct with the prisoner and the evidence, showed up to take a look at the goods.

"Wow!" exclaimed Daddy-O. "This motherfucker was on full! I ain't never seen this much dope."

"Hey, buddy," started Clark. "You need to be pattin' yourself on the back. If it wasn't fer that fine piece of undercover work, we never would've found this."

"Thanks, man," said Daddy-O.

"What do you think the street value of this is?" Slickster asked Fordham.

"Oh, it's got to be in the millions. Just off the top of my head? Maybe nine or ten million."

"Somebody's gon' have to die for this, I'm sure," said Too Sweet.

"They may already have," replied Fordham.

CHANDLER PARK DRIVE

TWENTY-FIVE

LEFTY AND CLARK ARRIVED AT THE Chicago lab in three hours, thirty-seven minutes flat, doing about 90 miles-per-hour all of the way.

"This shouldn't take that long," said Clark. "You can stay in the car while I take care of it," he added.

"Sounds like a winner to me," replied Lefty. He was, especially, fatigued from the ride, as he had driven the entire distance non-stop.

Clark removed the 80 lb. Satchel from the trunk and took it inside. Less than 20 minutes later, he exited the building with a big smile on his face, still carrying the satchel. He placed the bag back in the trunk.

"It's allll good," exclaimed Clark, as he re-entered the car.

"We're not gonna leave it here?" inquired Lefty.

"No. That was the whole point of us getting it tested so quickly. The boss wants to do a photo op with it tomorrow."

"Oh yeah, you're right. I'll tell you what, though. You're gonna have to drive this thing back tonight, 'cause I'm dog tired." It was now approaching 1 A.M.

"Ain't neither one of us gon' be drivin' tonight. We gon' camp out at the motel until about five or six in the mornin'. Hell, why not? The government's pickin' up the tab."

"But ..." started Lefty.

"Don't worry about the dope. We can take it in the room with us like it's a piece of luggage. You didn't think I was gon' suggest that we leave it in the car, did ya?"

"Well, I guess that'll be okay."

"As long as we're on the road by seven, we'll be back in Detroit in plenty enough time for the noon news."

Clark recommended that they stay at the Hampton Inn just outside of Chicago, citing that he'd stayed overnight there before. They had no problems getting accommodations there. They slept in adjoining rooms, for privacy's sake. Clark kept the satchel in the room with him.

After Clark received his six o'clock wake-up call, he rang Lefty's room at six-fifteen. The duo was dressed and ready to hit the road by six-fifty. They arrived at the Federal Building in Detroit at eleven-fifteen. To Fordham's delight, he was presented with the lab reports that indicated that the dope was of high quality, as well as the cache of drugs, itself. The news conference served as a boost for local law enforcement and the feds, alike. It was symbolic of how beneficial to the community at large, joint collaborations, such as this

CHANDLER PARK DRIVE

one were. In attendance were Fordham, the Detroit Chief of Police, Slickster, the Wayne County Prosecutor, and the U.S. District Attorney.

The reporters bombarded them with questions, while the cameramen snapped photos of the dope and money from various angles. One reporter, a cute young sister by the name of Kimberly Craig asked what, if any, impact the seizure would have on the deadly Detroit drug market.

"Significant," responded Fordham. "We believe that this seizure has seriously crippled a dangerous organization that has, up until this point, managed to deal illicit drugs in this community with relative impunity."

Ms. Craig's question and Fordham's response seemed to sum it all up, as a short time thereafter, the fanfare had ended and the lights and cameras were gone.

Considering how Lefty and Clark were gracious enough to volunteer to take the drugs to the lab to have it tested, he got two of the other crew members to return it for storage. He also gave the crew the next two days off for a job well done. Slickster followed suit and allowed his crew to take the rest of the week off, too, if they wanted it. It would be the following Monday before they'd be united again.

MICHAEL LEE

TWENTY-SIX

THURSDAY, DENARD WAS AT HOME relaxing when he received a telephone call from a young officer that worked the dayshift at Narcotics Prisoner Processing Unit answering the telephone.

"May I speak with Officer Blake?"

"Speaking," said Denard.

"Hey, how are you doing, Daddy-O? This is Bullet. Officer Watson at the base."

"Oh yeah, I know you. What's goin' on?"

"I hate to bother you at home, man, but this guy has called here twice from the county jail and his lawyer called once. They say that it's extremely important that you get in touch with the guy today."

"What's his name?"

"Javontay Sims."

"Yeah, I know exactly who he is. What did he say that he wants?"

"He didn't. He just said that he needed to talk to you today."

"What's his attorney's number?"

"It's…"

CHANDLER PARK DRIVE

"Hold on," said Denard. "Let me get a pen and some paper. Okay. Go ahead."

"His attorney's name is Jefferson Brogdon. He said that he can be reached at 109-3368, 313 area code."

"Alright. Thanks a lot."

Denard dialed the telephone number, while at the same time tried to figure out what Javontay Sims wanted with him. The phone rang only twice before it was answered.

"This is Jeff Brogdon. May I help you?"

"Hi. This is Officer Denard Blake. I'm returning your call."

"Hey, hey, how you doin, Officer Blake? First, let me say thank you for promptly responding to my call. I'll get straight to the point, 'cause I don't have a lot, and I don't want to waste your time. Anyway, my client was arrested by you and your crew and I'm representing him on those cases."

"Yeah, he's got a felonious assault on a police officer and a drug delivery case."

"Right, right. Well, my client wants to make a deal."

"Unless he's talking about giving up a real major player, I can't see us cuttin' no deal with your client counselor."

"Believe me when I tell you that he's got some information on a major player. Look, I don't want to try to conduct this type of business over the phone. Do you think you can meet me at the county jail in, say about, an hour? He can tell you much better than I can."

"Alright. I'll meet you in the lobby. I'll be bringing my boss with me. If for some unforeseen reason I can't make it, how can I reach you?" inquired Denard.

"Just call me at this number. That's my cell phone."

"Okay. I'll see you later."

Denard quickly telephoned Slickster. He was in luck. Slickster was at home chillin', too.

"Hello."

"Hey, boss. This is Denny. Did I call you at a bad time?"

"No, not at all. I guess I can find a minute or two to talk to you, brother."

"Cool. I just got off the phone with Javontay Sims' lawyer. He says that Javontay wants to cut a deal."

"Javontay Sims," pondered Slickster. "Isn't that the guy that pulled the gun on Jason?"

"Exactly."

"Well, what is he offering us?"

"That's just it. The lawyer didn't want to talk about it over the phone. He asked if we could meet him at the county jail within the hour. He wasn't specific, but he said that it was pretty big and it was time sensitive."

"What did you tell him?"

"I told him that I would get in touch with you, and we'd meet him down there."

CHANDLER PARK DRIVE

"Okay, I'll slip on some shoes and meet you down there. As cold as it is outside, leave it to you to get me out in this weather."

"Thanks, boss. Worst case scenario is we reject his offer and go back home."

"Okay, worst case scenario, I'll see you there."

The parking around the county jail was atrocious. It was visiting hours for the in-mates, and payday for the deputies. Once Denard had found a space, he entered the 7-story gray brick structure with the 4" wide windows. Slickster and the attorney were waiting, engaged in light-hearted cop-lawyer banter.

Jefferson Brogdon was a middle-aged brother with short wavy hair; partially gray. He wore wire-rimmed glasses, and had a thick, distinguished moustache. He was well dressed, carrying a Coach briefcase with a shoulder strap. Denard approached the two gentlemen.

"You must be Mr. Brogdon," said Denard as he extended his right hand.

"Just call me Jeff, brother. I was just tellin' your sergeant here that I don't usually take this kind of case, but Javontay's grandmother is a member of my father's church. So, I'm handling this pro bono. Anyway, I advised the young fella that he needs to figure out a way to cut himself a deal and the next thing I know he calls me with what sounds like some pretty heavy weight stuff. But he can tell you all about that."

After Denard and Slickster secured their weapons, the trio embarked on the visiting room located on the floor where Javontay is housed. A deputy escorted Javontay to the small, soundproof room. Only a thick glass window separated the visitors from the inmates. They communicated with each other by depressing buttons that activated an intercom system. Javontay was wearing a green, two-piece, wrinkled, pajama type outfit, and some tan rubber sandals. His hair was unkempt.

"Javontay," began Brogdon. "I have talked to Officer Blake, whom I'm sure you already know, and this is his sergeant, Mr. Kennedy. This is the deal. They can't make any promises right now, but if they are interested in what you have to offer, they have agreed to speak highly on your behalf to the prosecutor."

"Is that gon' get me out from up under dis case?" Javontay asked.

"Listen, brother, as your attorney, I strongly advise you to deal with these brothers. Neither I, nor anyone else for that matter, can promise you that you won't do any time. But I will promise you that if these officers act on your information and it turns out good for them, that I'll negotiate the least amount of time that you'll likely serve. You've got to remember, they do have a very strong case against you, and I'm just a lawyer, not Jesus."

"Okay, man, I'm trusting you, man."

"Thank you. Now go ahead. Tell them what you told me."

"It's like dis. I bunk up wit' dis eastside white boy that I used to gamble wit' back in da day. He slangin' a li'l dis and a li'l dat now. Dat's how he caught his case, too. Anyway, me and him been kickin' it right? He tell me that his older brother is 'bout to cop, like, 50 keys of raw. I'm jus' like thinkin' he bullshittin' until I heard him talkin' on the phone to his brother. They was tryin' to be all slick and shit 'cause they know these lines is tapped, but from what I got from them conversatin' is that the shit is 'posed to go down tomorrow at his brother's clubhouse in Detroit. His brother 'posed to be one of them motorcycle motherfuckers."

"What's his brother's name?" inquired Slickster.

"I dunno," said Javontay. "Ol' boy in here, his name is Jimmy. Jimmy Malloy. Can't y'all do some of that ol' fancy ass detective police shit and figure out who his brother is?"

"Yeah, Javontay, we'll try some of that fancy detective shit," mocked Denard. "Anyway, is that all you got?"

"Is that all? That ain't enough?"

"No, that's plenty, Javontay," replied Slickster. "As a matter of fact, if you think of anything else, let your lawyer know."

"I will, man, but y'all need to jump all over dis shit, man 'cause I know dis white boy ain't lyin' about dis shit."

"Gentlemen," interjected Brogdon. "I think we can conclude this little meeting. I'll talk to you tomorrow, Javontay."

Once they were rid of the attorney, Denard and Slickster obtained Jimmy Malloy's birthdate from sheriff's deputies, and later discussed a strategy in the comfort of Slickster's Cadillac.

MICHAEL LEE

"This is what I want you to do," said Slickster. "Go over to the Federal Building and run Jimmy Malloy in the L.E.I.N., N.C.I.C., and the Secretary of State; every database you can. See if you can find information on siblings. Have Gang Squad run his name through the Juvenile Information System to see if they've got anything on him. Also, have Gang Squad to give you a list of all white motorcycle clubs that operates clubhouses in Detroit. It'll probably be on the eastside. If you run into a dead end there, check with Vice. I'm going to contact Clark and see if those guys want in on this. We could use the extra manpower if this thing pans out. Call me if you find out anything significant."

It took Denard all of two hours to discover that Jimmy Malloy had one prior felony conviction and a juvenile record. Gang Squad had arrested him twice. The first time was for truancy and the second time was for violating the curfew. On that occasion, his older brother, Eddie, picked him up from the station. Gang Squad, 4 years earlier, listed Eddie as an associate in the Anarchists Motorcycle Club, based on the eastside of Detroit. Eddie had two prior arrests for narcotic-related offenses, but no convictions. The most interesting information that he discovered, though, was that the Anarchists' clubhouse had been targeted for drug raids two months earlier, but had never been raided.

Denard relayed his findings to Slickster, who concurred that the allegation warranted further investigation. Jason and Denard were ordered to conduct surveillance on the location, in hopes of developing probable cause for a search warrant.

CHANDLER PARK DRIVE

Unfortunately, he was unable to contact Clark who, like his fellow crewmembers, was probably enjoying the time off that their boss had granted them. He decided that if he were to raid the place, he'd seek help from within the Detroit Police Department.

MICHAEL LEE

TWENTY-SEVEN

IT WAS FRIDAY MORNING AND Denard had convinced a reluctant magistrate at 36th District Court to authorize a search warrant for the motorcycle club. He met up with the rest of his crew at the base by eleven o'clock. Everyone was suiting up and waiting for officers from the Tactical Services Section to arrive, as they were going to assist in the raid. Slickster was seated at his desk looking over the search warrant when Commander Jones walked up.

"Sgt. Kennedy, have your guys stand down, I need you and Daddy-O to meet me in my office, immediately," said the commander.

"Yes, sir," replied Slickster. "Let's go Daddy-O."

When they entered the commander's office, the commander, Stan Fordham, and two other clean-cut, middle-aged, white men with suits were present. One of the two strangers began speaking first.

"Gentlemen, thanks for coming. My name is Philip Malinowski, and this is Vernon Parrot. We're special agents with the F.B.I. and we investigate allegations of public corruption. It has come to our attention that an individual that you all have been working with has been engaged in illegal activity. Specifically, this individual has been stealing narcotic evidence and selling it on the street."

"Well, who is this individual?" inquired Slickster.

"It's Special Agent Kevin Clark," replied Malinowski.

Slickster and Daddy-O responded in shock and disbelief. The commander and Fordham's response was more subdued as they had been told minutes earlier.

"A little while back, we got a tip from an informant that Clark was engaged in this alleged activity. This particular informant had given us credible information in the past, so the matter bore investigating. Anyway, the allegation was that Clark would steal confiscated dope and sell it on the street. The informant said that Clark would switch the real dope with fake stuff after it had already been lab tested."

"Whaaat?" sighed Daddy-O.

"Yeah, this informant was pretty detailed. Anyway, there appeared to be some substance to the informant's story, so we got a few wire taps authorized and sporadically tailed Clark."

"So, how do we figure into this?" asked an anxious Daddy-O.

"I was getting to that," responded Malinowski. "We tapped the line of a guy that Clark, mainly deals to, an Eddie Malloy. Eddie told his brother, who is in the county jail about some big deal that's supposed to go down today, but he was real careful not to say too much. Well, we already knew about the deal. See, a couple of days ago, Clark took thirty-nine kilos of heroin to Chicago to be lab tested. While his partner was asleep in the hotel room, Clark placed a dummy bag in the car, which was to be returned to Chicago for storage, and ultimately to be destroyed, since the perpetrator, Stone, is dead. We've already tested the fake stuff. The informant is the one that told us when and where it's going down. Oh, and by the way, we're looking real hard at Clark for Stone's murder."

"What makes y'all think he did Stone? I was the one making buys from that guy," remarked Daddy-O.

"Well, we're looking at motive and opportunity. According to our informant, Clark is very selective about the dope that he steals, opting primarily for large amounts, but also for dope in cases that are resolved quickly. What quicker way to close a case than by the death of the defendant? Secondly, it just so happens that we did have a tail on him the night Stone was killed, but Clark managed to shake the tail."

All of the men listened attentively, but shook their heads in disgust and disbelief.

"I'm sorry," said Malinowski. "I digressed again. That's not why you're here. Each day we've been checking Eddie's brother's and his brother's bunkmate's visitors' list, and guess whose names showed up this morning?"

"Ours," replied Slickster.

"When we realized that you'd visited Sims yesterday, with his lawyer present, we figured Sims was

CHANDLER PARK DRIVE

rattin' somebody out. Well, lo and behold, your commander tells us that you did, in fact, secure a search warrant for the motorcycle club."

"Wow. That's deep," said Daddy-O.

"Gentlemen, once we realized how potentially volatile this situation could have been, we felt obligated to enlighten you. Now, we're not asking you not to execute your search warrant. We just want to work together with you to coordinate this properly."

"Absolutely," chimed Fordham. "This is one of my guys, so this devastates me personally. I'll offer you any kind of assistance that I can."

"We do have a little bit of time. According to our informant, he and Clark are supposed to meet with Eddie at the clubhouse at three o'clock this afternoon," said Parrot.

"So your informant is partnered with Clark in these dirty deeds?" inquired Daddy-O.

"Yeah, you can say that," said Parrot. "He'll be inside wearing a wire when the swap takes place."

"Why is the informant snitching on 'em?" asked Daddy-O.

"Greed," replied Malinowski. "Clark was giving him a ten percent cut, we're gonna pay him twenty. The guy was totally up front about his motivation. Well, anyway, if you all don't mind, we'd like to participate in your briefing."

"No problem at all," said Commander Jones.

At this point, Daddy-O's pager sounded. He looked at it and saw that it was Kathy's telephone number followed by '911'. The meeting broke up a short time thereafter. Denard returned to his work area to call Kathy back.

"Hello," she said.

"Hi, sweetness. This is Denny. What's the big emergency?"

"Is everything alright with you?" she asked.

"Yeah, why do you ask?"

"Well, you're not gonna believe what happened."

"What?"

"Are you somewhere that you can talk, privately?"

"Well, I'm at work and we're getting ready to go through a door, but I guess I can talk."

Slickster interrupted Denard's telephone conversation and told him that the commander wanted a word with the two of them in his office.

"Hey, listen, baby," said Daddy-O. "I've got to go to my boss's office for a quick meeting. Can I call you back later?"

"Sure. But don't forget."

"I won't. See ya later."

"Bye-bye."

The meeting in the commander's office was scaled back this time. Only Denard and Slickster were present.

"Listen, guys," said the commander. "I just wanted to speak to you two guys about this situation away from all of those federal agents. Slick, you and your crew chief, here, are going to have to bring the rest of your crew up to speed on this thing. Whenever a police officer is busted by a fellow police officer, especially one known to him or her, it can be stressful for all parties involved. I don't want your people to second guess themselves or be apprehensive about arresting Clark if it comes to that. They have to understand that they have to treat him the exact same way that they would treat any other criminal under the same circumstances. If you all catch Clark, he's gonna be desperate, just like a wounded animal. Don't be surprised if he tries to fire on one of you. Just make sure that your people understand that Clark is a criminal, and they are not to hesitate to take whatever action is appropriate to the situation. I don't want anything happening to any of you. Understood?"

"Yes, sir." Said Slickster.

"Understood, boss," replied Denard.

Slickster and Denard did as the commander said and gave the rest of the crew the heads-up. Denard pulled Jason to the side for a personal tête-à-tête regarding the situation.

"You know," said Denard, "it's ironic that we're out here chasin' these young, black thugs around tryin' to get this dope off the streets, while at the same time, we got some white, college-educated, law enforcement officer puttin' it right back out there."

"Yeah, you're right. That is kinda fucked up. What you gonna do, though. That's life."

"Yeah, I know. Anyway, man, you know what? I've been thinkin'. Those feds said that they've been tailing Clark and tapped his phone, right?"

"Okay. And?" inquired Jason.

"Well, think about it. They didn't know who was or was not involved in Clark's little scheme. I'll bet you a dollar to a doughnut that they were probably following some of us, too."

"You think so?"

"Hell yeah. Think about it. It was around the time that we started working with the feds that I started getting' this funny feelin' that I was being watched or something. I mentioned it to you, remember?"

"Yeah, okay. You may have said something to me along those lines."

"Well, anyway, that would explain it, and it makes perfect sense to me."

"I don't know," said Jason. "You could be right. I just think your ass was just paranoid. Look, we're gonna be briefing pretty soon. Let's get ready."

CHANDLER PARK DRIVE

TWENTY-EIGHT

KEVIN CLARK WAS STILL AT HOME preparing himself for what promises to be his biggest haul yet. He looked at the display of his ringing cell phone and saw that it was Red.

"What's goin' on, Red?" he asked.

"I'm jus' makin' sho' we still on fo' today, man."

"Listen, Red, I don't know why I agreed to let your ass go with me this time anyway, but don't keep callin' and buggin' me about this shit. We're on. Meet me at the spot at three-thirty and don't be late. I need you to help me carry the stuff."

"Aye aye, boss man. What if ol' Eddie try to pull some shit, what we gon' do?

"Shit like what?"

"You know. Some ol' bullshit, like tryin' to rob us or sump'n. Shit, or even worse than dat. What if dat sucker try to smoke us?"

"Look, man. I've been doin' business with Eddie for a while now and he ain't never came across like that to me, but if he does, you just hit the deck 'cause I'm definitely gon' give Mr. Eddie a lethal case of lead poisonin'".

"What about me? You ain't got no heat you can give me?"

"Hell no. That's all I'd need is two shady characters with guns in there. And Red, you had better not show up with a gun either or all bets are off, you understand?"

"Damn, man, you're hard on a nigga."

"Now, let me go over a couple of ground rules for you, Red. First of all, don't say nothin' other than hi and bye, understand?"

"Hi and bye, gotcha," replied Red.

"Secondly, you follow my lead. If I say it's time to go, then we go whether we got the money or not. Last but not least, if thangs go bad and we, somehow, get caught with this shit, you keep your mouth shut, hear?"

"C'mon man, what you think I am, a snitch?"

"Red, this ain't no jokin' matter. If we do this thang right today, we both are gonna be pretty well off for a while, so keep your bullshittin' down to a minimum."

"Damn, man, chill da fuck out. I was jus' jokin'"

"I'll see you there, Red."

"See ya."

Slickster, his crew and the FBI met at the Ninth Precinct on Gratiot. The briefing was long, but thorough. The Anarchists Motorcycle Club was on

CHANDLER PARK DRIVE

Grinnell, off Gratiot, so they were close enough that they could move when it was time to move.

Slickster and his crew were suited up in their van awaiting word from the FBI that it was time to move in on the target. The FBI, six agents total; four were paired up in two dark sedans, each one wearing thick, waist length jackets with the letters F-B-I on the backs. The other two were doing surveillance on the target location in SUV's. It was about three-fifteen when the occupants in the raid van heard the first radio transmission from the FBI.

"Primary to Slickster," said the voice over the radio.

"You got the Slickster," replied Kennedy.

"FYI. We got action at the target spot."

"10-4," said Slickster.

"We got two white males, biker types entering the location. One is carrying a briefcase. The other unlocked the front door with a key."

"10-4," said Slickster.

"That must be Eddie Malloy," said F.A.

"You think?" replied Pounder. Everyone laughed.

"You guys knock it off," said Slickster. "I need to be able to hear this radio."

Ten minutes later, they received another update.

"Okay," said the voice over the radio. "we've got two vehicles just pulled up in the parking lot. Both are occupied one time; one is salt the other is pepper. Be advised, though, the pepper is a friendly. I repeat. The pepper is a friendly."

MICHAEL LEE

"10-4," replied Slickster.

"What they mean by friendly?" asked Jason.

"That means he's their CI," replied Denard. "Shhhhhh. Be quiet."

"They're carrying two duffel bags. The salt is definitely our target. They're at the door knockin'. Okay, they're in. We'll let you know."

"10-4," said Slickster.

The inside of the motorcycle club was dark and chilly. There was a DJ's booth, a dance floor with a chrome pole in the middle, two six-foot pool tables, some tables and chairs, two bathrooms, a front door and a back door. Eddie was there with one of the club officers; his right-hand man Jeff. Jeff had an Uzi in his hand when Red and Clark entered.

"Let's do business, Biloxi Bob. What's happ'nin' Red? Bob finally decided to cut you in on some of the action, huh? Since you did introduce me to him and all."

"Look, man, let's just get this shit over with," said Clark.

Eddie turned the light on over one of the pool tables, while Jeff stood back in the shadows. Eddie put the briefcase on top of the table and Red and Clark did the same with the duffel bags. Eddie counted the bricks first before stabbing one of the bricks with a buck knife and snorting the residue from the blade. He closed his eyes and swayed for a few seconds before speaking.

CHANDLER PARK DRIVE

"That's some good shit, Bob. Some real good shit. Now what did we say? Oh yeah, that's right, you want ten per, right? Now, let's see; ten per times thirty-nine is three-hundred ninety thousand, ain't it?"

"Eddie, don't play games with me," said Clark.

"I'm just funnin', Bob. Take your money," said Eddie as he slid the briefcase across the table to Clark, who commenced counting.

After the foursome had been inside of the building together for less than fifteen minutes, the radio sounded off again.

"Move in!" yelled the surveillance crew. "The deal is down! Move in!"

"We're rollin'" replied Slickster.

With the two FBI cars in tow, Slickster and his crew raced to the motorcycle club. The uniformed officers and the FBI took up positions outside, as Slickster and crew forced their way inside. Pounder had the front door open with just three swings of the battering ram. Denard was the shotgun man.

"Police! Search warrant!" they all yelled as they entered the dark building. At this point, the only light inside was the one that shined from the flashlight mounted atop Denard's shotgun. Almost immediately they encountered gunfire, as they heard the rat-a-tat-tat sounds and saw the muzzle flash in the far, left corner of the building. Denard trained his weapon in that area, illuminating the silhouette of a gunman. He didn't hesitate to begin firing the shotgun in that direction.

Before he'd realized what he'd done, he'd racked and released three rounds from the pump action 12-Gauge shotgun. The rat-a-tat-tat sound had stopped. The stench of gunpowder was in the air. The dense gun smoke was looming about.

They found Eddie hiding in the women's room, Red was cowering underneath the pool table, and one of the uniforms stopped Clark as he tried to flee via the back door. Jeff was in the far, left corner of the building, still holding the Uzi, but mortally wounded by a shotgun blast to the face, throat and left thigh. Blood and steam poured from his wounds. The blood splattered much of the wall, and Jeff had no discernible features left in his face. All of the money and dope was still on the pool table. Slickster did a quick survey and determined that everyone on his team was unharmed.

Slickster got on the radio and called for an ambulance for Jeff before announcing to all of the folks on the outside assignments that the inside was secured. The FBI entered to find the three living occupants lined up and facing a wall. Too Sweet was just about to search Clark when a FBI agent walked up to them.

"I'll take him from here," said the FBI agent.

"But I," started Too Sweet.

The FBI agent interrupted him, saying, "Listen Officer. I *said* we'll take him from here. Now, what part of that don't you understand?"

Too Sweet cringed, as the agent handcuffed Clark and led him out of the building. They also took Red and Eddie, leaving Slickster and his crew behind to process

CHANDLER PARK DRIVE

evidence and the crime scene until the Homicide detectives and other big shots arrived.

Considering he'd just killed someone for the first time in his career, Denard seemed to be taking it well. Each of his crewmembers praised him for a job well done, and assured him that he could talk to them if he needed. After all of the evidence technicians' camera flashes had stopped, the dead body had been removed, reports had been completed, and evidence collected, Denard could only think of the comforts of home.

TWENTY-NINE

KEVIN CLARK FOUND HIMSELF BEING led into the Federal Building downtown by two FBI agents, in handcuffs. They spent their time in the car trying to establish a rapport with him. He knew the drill, for he had ran it himself on so many other suspects in the past. He just sat silently, ignoring them while contemplating his dismal future. They had him handcuffed to the rear, as they sat him down in a small room with a table, two chairs, no windows, and one door. He was left alone for about twenty minutes when Special Agent Malinowski returned carrying a beige folder with papers inside.

"Hi Kevin. I'm Phil Malinowski. Well, Kevin, it looks like you've gotten yourself into a bit of a predicament here," said Malinowski. "I won't lie to you and tell you that you aren't going to prison. You're going. The question is, for how long. Now, you have a right to sit there and say nothing at all. I'll grant you that. The problem with that is that you'll be leaving it up to people like Red, Eddie, me, and not to mention, the evidence to tell your story. Kevin, you've got to know by now that we're not going to portray you in the most favorable of lights. So what I'm saying, Kevin, is this, I can be your best friend throughout this ordeal or I can be your worst enemy. Which one is it going to be?"

Kevin sat quietly, staring at the stone floor beneath his feet. He digested the monologue that had just been delivered. Even though he knew that the agent had just performed a textbook Interrogation 101 technique, it still sounded pretty damned good. After pondering the offer for a moment, he looked up from the floor and asked Malinowski, "What do you want me to do?"

Malinowski said, "Look, man, I know how difficult this must be for you. I've got your personnel file right here. Heck, you're highly decorated, well trained, southern bred, and college-educated. Not to mention, you've got a supportive family at home. No, I'm not trying to make this more painful for you than it has to be. All I want from you is the truth."

"The truth, huh?" asked Clark.

"That's it. All I want is the truth."

"And the truth shall make me free," said Clark, sarcastically.

"I don't know about free, Clark, but if you help me wrap this thing up quickly, I can certainly speak on your behalf to cushion the blow a bit."

Clark sighed heavily. He stared into space and shook his head. "Okay. I'll tell you everything you want to know."

"Just a minute, Clark, let me get a tape recorder before you start talking."

"No," said Clark, "if you want a statement from me, I'll write it out and you can videotape me writing it if you want. Don't worry. I'll be sure to sign it, too. Plus, I want to get these damned handcuffs off."

"No problem," replied Malinowski.

Malinowski left the room and returned a few minutes later to set up a tripod and videotape recorder. Before seating himself across the table again from Clark, he took the handcuffs off and gave Clark a pad of paper and an ink pen. Clark took about thirty minutes to complete the statement before he handed it over to Malinowski. He carefully perused the document before asking Clark a few additional questions.

"So let me get this right, you *did* shoot Stone, huh?"

"That's what I wrote, ain't it."

"What kind of gun did you use?"

"Oh, it was a little two shot derringer I picked up on a raid a few years back. A thirty-two caliber."

"Where is the gun right now?"

Clark paused. He looked at Malinowski, and then he looked at the camera, before hanging his head down again.

"Clark, where is the gun now? I should tell you Clark that, as we speak, one of the other agents is typing up a search warrant for your house so that we can try to find that gun. Now, I know you don't want us going to your house, tearing things up and frightening your family, do you? So, why don't you just tell me where it is to save us all a lot of heartache."

CHANDLER PARK DRIVE

Clark was sobbing now. He said, "Okay, okay. I'll tell you where it is." He wiped the tears from his eyes and regained his composure. "Have y'all already told my wife what's happened?"

"No. We were going to let you do that, Kevin."

"I can't brang myself to. Would you, at least, call her and let her know what's happened for me? I'd appreciate it."

"Sure thing, Clark. Now, where's the gun?"

"It's locked up in my desk drawer upstairs ... on the twenty-sixth floor."

Malinowski thanked Clark and got up to leave the room.

"Phil," started Clark, "be sure to tell Red that I can't believe he did this to me. I know it was him."

Without responding, Malinowski left the room to check out the claim. Less than thirty seconds later, he heard a muffled, yet loud popping sound come from the room that Clark was in. He, and other agents, ran back inside, to find Clark slumped over the arm of his chair with blood pouring from his mouth, a large hole in the back of his head, and hair with brain matter splattered against the wall. A two-shot derringer was lying on the floor at his feet.

All of the agents responded in shock and disbelief. The videotape recorder was still running and had captured the image of Clark unzipping his pants and reaching into his crotch area to retrieve the gun, which he stuck in his mouth before squeezing the trigger. The agent that handcuffed Clark immediately realized that he'd done a piss poor job of searching him.

MICHAEL LEE

When Denard made it home, he realized that he couldn't remember driving there. He was lethargic. It was as if the car had been on automatic pilot. His thoughts were consumed with images of the dead man's body. Taking another man's life is more than a notion, he thought.

As he got out of his car and was walking toward the front door of his house, a white man with a suit and tie on exited a car across the street and approached him. Denard assumed that he was one of the FBI agents.

"Excuse me, sir," said the man. "You're Officer Blake, right?"

"That's right," said Denard.

"Here you are, sir," the man said, as he gave Denard a large manila envelope and proceeded to walk away.

"Wait a minute. What is this?"

"I don't know," said the man, "all I know is you're being sued."

Sued, thought Denard. *They usually serve those things at the base*, he rationalized. He went inside and tossed his keys and cap on the dining room table and commenced to tearing open the envelope. He was devastated by the first words that he saw in the middle of the first page. They were, 'Sheila Blake vs. Denard Blake'. It took him to read a few more lines to realize that she was seeking a divorce. He threw the papers down and ran through the house. He hadn't even noticed that her car wasn't there. He checked all of the rooms and discovered that all of her personal belongings

CHANDLER PARK DRIVE

were gone. He felt dejected and empty; as though a gaping hole was in his heart.

He collected the document from the floor and sat down at the dining room table to read it. There were many unanswered questions, but since Michigan was a no-fault divorce state, Sheila didn't have to specify in her complaint why she wanted one; irreconcilable differences would suffice.

Denard was dazed. He suddenly remembered that Kathy had something important that she wanted to talk to him about. He called her from his cell phone.

"Hello," she said.

"Hey, sweetie. This is Denard. When you called earlier, what did you want to talk to me about?"

"Have you talked to your wife?"

"No. Why?"

"Well, some lady called here today and told me that she hopes that I'm happy and that I could have your ass. When I asked who it was, she said that she was your wife."

Denard just held his forehead in his hand, with his eyes closed, shaking his head for several seconds.

"Hey, baby," whispered Kathy, "are you there? Are you alright?"

"Yeah, yeah, I'm alright. Let me talk to you later, baby."

He hung up the phone and slammed it on the table, knocking aside his baseball cap. There was another large white envelope on the table with his name handwritten in Sheila's writing on it. Printed on the top left corner of the envelope were the words, 'Dukes

Private Investigations, LLC'. Denard took out the envelope's contents. Wow, he thought to himself. All the while he thought he had Sheila fooled, she was fooling him. Unbeknownst to him, she suspected his philandering and had hired a private eye to follow him around. The envelope contained a number of photographs of him and Kathy together, including one of him kissing her at the front door of her apartment building. Sheila left a short note inside that read as follows:

Denard, I hope this woman makes you happier than I could. I've taken the next two weeks off work, so please don't try to get in touch with me. As far as the house and the other property goes, my attorney will be in touch with you. Have a nice life. I'll see you around. Maybe.

A tear rolled down his face just as his home telephone rang.

"Hello," he said.

"Yo, what's up, dog?" asked Jason.

"Nothin'," sighed Denard.

"Hey man, did you hear what happened?"

"No, what?"

"Man, where have you been? That shit is all over the news. Clark killed his self at the FBI headquarters downtown."

"What?"

"Yep, man, and check this out. While we were at the motorcycle club, Two Sweet said that one of those

CHANDLER PARK DRIVE

arrogant feebies took Clark away from him before he could search him good."

"Damn, that's fucked up. Oh well. Another one bites the dust."

"I'm sorry, man. I wasn't thinking. I know you probably don't want to hear about this shit. I completely forgot about what you've already been through today. Listen, man, I'm gonna let you relax and clear your mind with that beautiful wife of yours. Tell her I said hello, and y'all take care of each other, okay? Later, brother."

"Later."

To be continued ···

MICHAEL LEE

Sneak Preview
Of Michael C. Lee's next book, entitled
"Real Secrets Die"
Denard Blake (AKA Daddy-O) and Terrence Kennedy (AKA Slickster) are back !!!!!!!!!!!!!!!!!!

CHAPTER ONE

Rhonda was doing the new Booty Call hustle on the dance floor, while Nichelle was trying to have a good time. Rhonda had talked her in to going out tonight, despite Nichelle's insistence to just stay at home with the kid and watch TV or something. Nichelle would never have accepted an invitation out on the town from anyone else, but because Rhonda was her closest friend in the world, she relented. Nichelle had not yet gotten used to the idea that her husband of eight years was gone. No, he wasn't dead, she thought, but when that damned self-righteous-ass judge uttered the words, 'ten to fifteen', and slammed that gavel against that fucking oak, it sounded a hell of a lot more like a death sentence.

CHANDLER PARK DRIVE

Rhonda was just doing what any good friend would do. She was trying to help Nichelle get on with her life.

Nonetheless, Nichelle still couldn't help but feel guilty. *How does it look to his family*, she thought. She's out painting the town, while he's on lockdown. And what about their son, Thelmon, Jr., how did *he* feel about being babysat by his daddy's family while mommy was out partying with Auntie Rhonda. Although it had already been six months, she wondered if she would *ever* adjust to life without Thelmon; life without sex.

Next, she found herself thinking about what *his* friends might think if *they* ran into her. Would they think she was a slut? Would they try to push up on her themselves? Would they run back and tell Thelmon lies about her? All of the uncertainty was destroying her. She sat there staring into what seemed like perpetual space, twirling the thin red plastic stirrer in her drink, a White Russian.

"Whew, Girl! That was fun," exclaimed Rhonda, snapping Nichelle out of the trance. "Next time, you better come on out there and get your groove on."

"I saw you out there. I don't know how to do that hustle. Hell, I *just* learned how to do that hustle that they used to do back in the day. You know the one," she said, while making circles with her index finger, nodding her head, smiling.

"Girl, I *know* you ain't talkin' about that hustle we used to do off of Stevie Wonder's 'My Eyes Don't Cry'."

"Yeah, girl. That's it. Why don't they do that one any more? Now, I'll get out there if they play that one."

Rhonda sucked her teeth, rolled her eyes and replied, "Girl, that song is so played out, it ain't funny. Where's that slow ass waitress? I want another drink. You ready for another one? I got it."

"Yeah, that'd be nice. I'll have another. You just missed the waitress. She made her rounds about thirty seconds before you came back."

"Well, I'm not waiting for her to come back. I'm going to the bar. You're drinking White Russian, right?"

Nichelle smiled and nodded her head. Rhonda pranced away with a confident strut. Even though she was the mother of a sixteen-year-old high school b-baller, this 36-year old dark chocolate sister *knew* that she was packing much back. Her son's friends still flirt and make goo-goo eyes at her, whenever her son isn't watching. The back-less Coogi dress that she was wearing was

CHANDLER PARK DRIVE

the perfect compliment to her curvaceous figure. At 5'7", 145 lbs., the 3" stilettos that she wore placed her at eye level to most of the men at the club.

It was Wednesday night in Detroit. Late July, 1998. Slight overcast seventy degrees. Flood's Bar and Grill wasn't just *the* place to be; it was the *only* place to be. As next door neighbor to the Blue Cross/Blue Shield Headquarters on Lafayette Avenue, it was a natural choice for Blue Cross/Blue Shield workers to gather for after-work affairs. Flood's was Detroit's premiere 'meet and greet' spot. It was one of the few places that most of Detroit's upscale blacks supported religiously. The club, with its brass, glass and mahogany design, and its eclectic art, featured some of the city's best jazz acts, hip-hop DJ's, and soul food. Tonight, the club was packed and the line outside was growing.

Nichelle, though her spirits were down, beamed in her red silk tee, red leather shorts, matching toenails and strappy sandals. She was a couple inches shorter than Rhonda, smaller, and high yellow.

Rhonda and Nichelle met each other four years earlier. Rhonda was hired in where Nichelle worked already, a Mariott Hotel in Dearborn.

MICHAEL LEE

They were customer service representatives. Since they were the only two blacks on their shift, and they were both from the eastside of Detroit, naturally they bonded. Before either one of them realized it, they were shopping together on off days, scheduling off days together, partying together, and sharing secrets with each other. Flood's became their favorite hangout.

Totally disregarding the long line of willing patrons, Terrence Kennedy flashed his badge to the bouncer, and walked in. The, newly promoted, Violent Crimes lieutenant had just finished up at 1300 Beaubien, Detroit Police Headquarters. Flood's was within walking distance and he was in desperate need of a drink. Today was, particularly rough. He responded to a scene on the eastside, where a 27-year old woman and her two children, aged seven and three were found dead inside their badly burned house. Their bodies were riddled with bullets. A real sloppy job that some heinous creep, or creeps, had done at covering up a murder, or in this case, a triple-murder.

As if the day wasn't going bad enough, his wife called to rag on him about working late again. They had only been married for three years, but the pressure seemed to be getting to her already.

CHANDLER PARK DRIVE

He thought that by waiting until he was thirty-seven years old to get married, that he'd bypass that type of foolishness. *Boy, was I wrong*, he thought. This wife of his complained about everything. If it wasn't the work hours, it was the garbage that he didn't take out. If not that, then something else. But he'd convinced himself that despite her eccentricities and complaints, she wasn't all that bad. After all, she was a hell of a dime piece for a 35-year old, plus she made good money selling flowers; owned her own floral shop on Coolidge in Oak Park.

Terrence had just made it past the dance floor when he looked over the brass railing and saw the most gorgeous woman that he'd laid his eyes on in a while. At 40, Terrence considered himself a looker, too. He was 6'4", a former University of Michigan point guard reserve, stocky build, brown skinned, salt and pepper fade, with a five o'clock shadow, Hugo Boss suit, Pangborn Tie. He ordered a Long Island Iced Tea from the barmaid, and attempted to provide the beauty across the room with a glimpse of his best feature; his perfect pearly whites. He smiled, but she didn't even notice him. *Damn*, he thought.

As he stared at her, he started to have the feeling that he knew her from somewhere. No, he was certain of it. He'd seen her somewhere before. He racked his brain trying to figure out where. Was it from there? Work? Was she a friend of his wife's? He couldn't figure it out. He wanted to approach her, but he was afraid that when he said, 'Excuse me, but don't I know you from somewhere?' she might erupt in laughter, thinking that that was the oldest and corniest pickup line in the book. He was certainly not going to approach her now that her dark-skinned girlfriend was back seated at the table with her. He had no desire to be the brunt of their jokes for the rest of the night, but he *had* to meet this woman. He finally decided that he would wait until the DJ played that song that was just right to ask her to dance. *Not too slow, not too fast*, he thought to himself. *Just right*.

"Drink up, girl," proclaimed Rhonda. "I'm half way finished with my second drink and you haven't even started on your second one yet."

"I know," responded Nichelle. "I was just thinking about Thelmon, Jr."

"Didn't you leave him with Thelmon's sister?"

"Yeah, but ..."

"But nothin', girl," said Rhonda, as she firmly put her drink down and placed her hand across the top of Nichelle's hand. "Now, tell the truth. Were you thinking about Thelmon, Jr. or Thelmon?"

"You know the answer," replied Nichelle, while avoiding eye contact with her friend. She sipped the remainder of her first drink, and sighed.

"Listen, girl. Look at me! I know how you must feel. I'd be devastated, too. Shit, and I know it don't help that Thelmon was ... *is* fine as all get back, but girl, you've got to keep your head up and be strong. I know that he wouldn't want you moping around like he was dead or something. Besides, you haven't given up on trying to get his conviction reversed, have you?"

"Of course not."

"Well, there you go. Where there's life, there's hope. In the meantime, girl, why don't you try living? *You're* not locked up, you know."

"Excuse me," said Terrence, who stood tableside, nursing a Long Island.

They both looked at him. "Yes?" remarked Rhonda.

*Always the one that I'm **not** interested in*, thought Terrence. He replied, "I was wondering if one of you two beautiful ladies would like to dance."

"Exc-uuusse me!" shouted the short, loud-mouthed, waitress, as she tried to navigate her way through the crowd, carrying a tray full of catfish nuggets and wing-dings. A younger white woman, with goddess braids, she looked slightly annoyed, as she waited for Terrence to allow her passage. He bladed his body, sucked in his stomach a bit, and pulled his drink toward his chest, as she bustled along.

"My girlfriend would love to," said Rhonda. The sound of Frankie Beverly and Maze's 'Joy and Pain' filled the room.

Nichelle tilted her head to the right and bucked her eyes at Rhonda, sipped from her empty glass and said, "Rhonda!"

"Thank me later, girl. Now go on before the song goes off. I'll stay here and watch your drinks," she said as she took Terrence's, practically empty, Long Island Iced Tea from his hand.

Delighted with the song and the dance partner, Terrence took the lead as they marveled onlookers with their ballroom skills. He and Nichelle danced as though they'd just practiced yesterday.

"Nice dancer," Terrence whispered in her ear during a turn.

CHANDLER PARK DRIVE

She smiled and said, "Thank you. You're not so bad yourself."

Joy and Pain ended, and a slow jam began. Terrence was delighted that Nichelle wanted to keep dancing, even though the pace had slowed considerably.

"So, what's your name?" he asked her.

"Nichelle. What's yours?"

"I'm Terrence." He was trying to figure out if he knew a Nichelle from somewhere, but the name just didn't ring a bell. "So, Nichelle, I've never seen you here before. Do you come here often?"

"I used to, but I haven't been here in a few months. Ya know, Terrence, you have got a very familiar face. Do I know you from somewhere?"

"Oh my God. You are not gonna believe this," said Terrence, grinning from ear to ear. "I was checking you out earlier and I was thinking the exact same thing about you, but I didn't want to come out and say it. You know. You might've thought I was trying to come on to you or something."

"No, I'm pretty sure I know you from somewhere," she replied. "I just can't put my finger on it, though."

Terrence refused to come straight out of the police bag yet. He was, actually, hoping that he didn't know her through his job. "Well, let's see," he said. "Let's try a little process of elimination. Are you married?"

"Yes, why?"

"I don't know. I was thinking that I might know your husband. What's his name?"

"I doubt that you know him. I know all of his friends, but anyway it's Thelmon."

"No, you're right. I don't know anybody by that name."

"How about you?" she inquired.

"Me what?"

"Married. Are you married?"

"Oh, I'm sorry, yes. Three years."

"You happy?" she asked.

"At times. How about you?" he asked.

"I guess you could say that." The song was ending. "Well, anyway. Thank you for the dance."

"No. Thank *you*," he replied. "Can I buy you a drink?"

"Sure. Why not."

Not wanting to appear to be too anxious, Terrence returned to the bar as she returned to her seat. He sat at the bar and wrote out a note on a

CHANDLER PARK DRIVE

napkin. He summoned a waitress, ordered drinks for Nichelle and Rhonda, and instructed the waitress to hand the note to Nichelle. He told her to keep the change from the twenty-dollar bill.

When the waitress returned to Nichelle and Rhonda's table with the drinks, slyly, she handed Nichelle the note. It read:

I was pleased to meet you. Can we do it again sometime? (313) 555-4253 Terrence

By the time she took her eyes off of the note, he was walking out of the door, but she was intrigued by everything about him, so far. She was certain that there was more to Terrence than meets the eye, and she couldn't wait to get to know him better.